THE COMING

OIL

CRISIS

IVOR MYERS

Remnant Publications, Coldwater, MI

Published by Remnant Publications, Inc.
649 E. Chicago Road
Coldwater, MI 49036
517-279-1304
www.remnantpublications.com

The author assumes full responsibility for the accuracy
of all facts and quotations as cited in this book.

Unless othewise noted, Scripture quotations are taken
from The Holy Bible, King James Version.

Scripture quotations marked (ESV) are from
The Holy Bible, English Standard Version® (ESV®),
Copyright © 2001 by Crossway, a publishing ministry of Good
News Publishers. Used by permission. All rights reserved.

Scripture quotations noted Contemporary English Version,
Copyright © 1991, 1992, 1995 by American
Bible Society, Used by Permission.

Cover designed by Eric Pletcher
Copy editing by Julia Bellman
Text designed by Greg Solie • AltamontGraphics.com

ISBN: 978-1-937718-34-3

Contents

ॐ

THIS BOOK IS DEDICATED TO

TWO PRECIOUS WOMEN IN MY LIFE.

ONE IS MY BRIDE, ATONTE.

THANK YOU FOR BEING

WHO YOU ARE. I LOVE YOU.

THE OTHER IS THE BRIDE OF CHRIST.

I PRAY THAT YOU WILL BE

ENCOURAGED TO ARISE AND SHINE.

I LOVE YOU TO

Chapter 1
A Crisis in Our Midst

By the year 2008, sixty of the ninety-eight oil-producing countries had reached their geological peak and were declining in their oil production.

In his book *Out of Gas: The End of the Age of Oil*, David Goodstein wrote:

> The world will soon start to run out of conventionally produced, cheap oil. If we manage somehow to overcome that shock by shifting the burden to coal and natural gas, the two other primary fossil fuels, life may go on more or less as it has been—until we start to run out of all fossil fuels by the end of this century. And by the time we have burned up all that fuel, we may well have rendered the planet unfit for human life. …

> Some say that the world supply of oil will last for another forty years or more, but that view is almost surely mistaken. The peak, which will occur when we've used half the oil nature made for us … will come far sooner than that. When the peak occurs, increasing demand will meet decreasing supply, possibly with disastrous results. [1]

We have entered an oil crisis that has continued to this day. Four signs point to this fact. First, as shown in the above quote, the rate of demand for oil is exceeding the rate of available supply. Second, as oil becomes scarce, prices for everything else goes up. This hike in prices will also naturally increase crime. Third, the rising cost of oil, and the dropping value of the dollar, makes travel more expensive and, therefore, more difficult. Finally the fourth, there is much talk of the need of looking into alternative sources of energy.

As serious as this issue is, this book is not about a literal oil crisis. The current oil crisis reflects an even deeper and infinitely more important crisis that is coming upon our planet. It is a crisis of a spiritual nature best summed up in the parable of the ten virgins found in Matthew 25.

---

1   David Goodstein, *Out of Gas: The End of the Age of Oil* (New York: W. W. Norton & Company, Inc., 2004), 15, 17.

> Then shall the kingdom of heaven be likened unto ten virgins, which took their lamps, and went forth to meet the bridegroom. And five of them were wise, and five were foolish. They that were foolish took their lamps, and took no oil with them: But the wise took oil in their vessels with their lamps. While the bridegroom tarried, they all slumbered and slept. And at midnight there was a cry made, Behold, the bridegroom cometh; go ye out to meet him. (Matthew 25:1–6)

This parable describes the spiritual condition of God's church just before the second coming of Jesus Christ. In it, ten virgins (professing Christians) go out to the meet the bridegroom (Jesus, at his second coming). Five are wise, and five are foolish. All ten have lamps, but only the wise have brought enough oil to last them until the coming of the bridegroom. There is a delay in the coming of the bridegroom, and all ten virgins fall asleep, only to be awakened by the warning that the bridegroom is coming. The following is what happens next:

> Then all those virgins arose, and trimmed their lamps. And the foolish said unto the wise, Give us of your oil; for our lamps are gone out. But the wise answered, saying, Not so; lest there be not enough for us and you: but go ye rather to them that sell, and buy for yourselves. And while they went to buy, the bridegroom came; and they that were ready went in with him to the marriage: and the door was shut. Afterward came also the other virgins, saying, Lord, Lord, open to us. But he answered and said, Verily I say unto you, I know you not. Watch therefore, for ye know neither the day nor the hour wherein the Son of man cometh. (Matthew 25:7–13)

The oil in this parable is symbolic of the Holy Spirit (see 1 Samuel 16:13; Zechariah 4). It is the spirit that causes the lamp to burn (Exodus 27:20). Thus where there is no Holy Spirit, there can be no light or fire. The lamp symbolizes the Word of God, and the truth it contains. "Thy word is a lamp unto my feet, and a light unto my path" (Psalm 119:105).

The parable is teaching that one may have knowledge of the truth, yet without the Holy Spirit, he or she will be unprepared for the return of Christ, represented by the Bridegroom. If we lack the Holy Spirit, we will be found unprepared for the crisis. Telltale signs show what we are headed for, and we are, in fact, already in an oil crisis.

The time is coming when demand for the Holy Spirit will exceed supply. Isaiah 55:6 warns, "Seek ye the Lord while he may be found, call upon him while he is near." "Everything in the world is in agitation. The signs of the times are ominous. Coming events cast their shadows before. The Spirit of God is withdrawing from the earth. ... The crisis is stealing gradually upon us" (*The Desire of Ages*, 636).

Crime in the church is also on the increase, for where there is a lack of Spirit, there is certain to be a lack of love. "Because iniquity shall abound, the love of many shall wax cold. But he that shall endure unto the end, the same shall be saved" (Matthew 24:12–13). In other words, the fire goes out, and the heart will grow cold. As we look around at the relationships within the church and behold the crimes of gossip, adultery, fornication, envy, suspicion, and jealousy on the increase, we may know that we are in an oil crisis.

Many take it for granted that they are Christians, simply because they subscribe to certain theological tenets. But they have not brought the truth into practical life. They have not believed and loved it, therefore they have not received the power and grace that come through sanctification of the truth. Men may profess faith in the truth; but if it does not make them sincere, kind, patient, forbearing, heavenly minded, it is a curse to its possessors, and through their influence it is a curse to the world. *(The Desire of Ages*, 309)

Even travel has been affected by this spiritual oil crisis. In the days of the early church, the news of the gospel had been taken to the whole then-known world. They had no modern-day mode of travel, no printing press, and no internet. Today we have all this to our avail, and yet the three angels' messages have yet to travel around the world. Since it is oil that fuels today's mode of travel, could it be that a lack of the Holy Spirit is preventing the message of truth traveling into the whole world? Could it be that the church is running on fumes?

The final sign of this oil crisis is all the talk of alternative sources of energy. Looking for something new—gimmicks, New Age ideas and philosophies, popular music, and feel-good messages to replace the work that only the Holy Spirit can do—is a futile exercise. It is only through a vital connection with Christ, through prayer and Bible study, that we may gain access to the divine Spirit of God (see John 4:23–24).

Prayer is the breath of the soul. It is the secret of spiritual power. *No other means of grace can be substituted*, and the health of the soul be preserved. Prayer brings the heart into immediate contact with the Well-spring of life, and strengthens the sinew and muscle of the religious experience. Neglect the exercise of prayer, or engage in prayer spasmodically, now and then, as seems convenient, and you lose your hold on God. The spiritual faculties lose their vitality; the religious experience lacks health and vigor.

It is only at the altar of God that we can kindle our tapers with divine fire. It is only the divine light that will reveal the littleness, the incompetence, of human ability, and give clear views of the perfection and purity of Christ. It is only as we behold Jesus that we desire to be like Him, only as we view His righteousness that we hunger and thirst to possess it; and it is only as we ask in earnest prayer, that God will grant us our heart's desire. (*Gospel Workers*, 254, 255, emphasis added)

For all who desire to follow Him, His example is left on record. Prayer sanctified His ministry. Strength and vigor for daily duty are derived from worshiping God in the beauty of holiness. *The lamp must be filled with holy oil before its light can shine amid the moral darkness.* (*The Signs of the Times*, October 31, 1900, emphasis added)

Our only hope is to drill—and drill now! We must desire a deeper experience in our prayer lives, and dig deeper in the Word of God. Satan has imposed a ban on prayer and Bible study for many of God's people, and it's time to lift this ban. We must get on our knees and drill. We are too satisfied with a shallow experience, a shallow prayer life, and shallow Bible study. Minutes of prayer will not do. A crisis is just before us.

There are strong temptations before us, sharp tests. The commandment-keeping people of God are to prepare for this time of trial by obtaining *a deeper experience* in the things of God and a practical knowledge of the righteousness of Christ. ... Not to unbelievers only, but to church members the words are spoken, *"Seek ye the Lord while he may be found, call ye upon him while he is near"* (Isaiah 55:6). (*In Heavenly Places*, 347, emphasis added}

Christ, our example, demonstrated that one must possess the oil *before* the crisis hits. Christ's victory on Calvary was obtained in the garden of Gethsemane. The word "Gethsemane" literally means "oil press," and it was in fact, located in the "Mount of Olives." According to the book of Exodus, the oil used for the lamp was obtained from "beaten" olives. "Thou shalt command the children of Israel, that they bring thee pure oil olive beaten for the light, to cause the lamp to burn always" (Exodus 27:20).

The olive groves were his sanctuary for prayer. There, secluded from every human eye, he communed with his Heavenly Father. His moral powers were strengthened by his meditation and communion with God. (*The Youth's Instructor*, September 1, 1873)

Could it be that Christ's agonizing prayer in the garden of Gethsemane in preparation for His final crisis was a demonstration of the kind of prayer it will take for us to be ready for our final crisis? Christ, the "beaten" Olive, was pressed in the Mount of Olives, the "olive press," and so filled with the Spirit that He overcame Satan and all his forces on Mount Calvary. It was this victory in Gethsemane that led to the light flowing from Calvary's cross.

The vision of Zechariah 4:1–6, shows two "olive trees," emptying oil into the candlestick. Could this vision be a revelation of how the man Jesus Christ, "the light of the world," was able to shine forth with such power, "not by might, nor by power" but by God's spirit received through his communion with his heavenly Father?

To the believing Jews in Jerusalem in the time of Christ, Olivet was a frequent resort for devotion. The hills and valleys about Jerusalem, now so bleak and bare, were then studded with olive-groves and orchards, and here the faithful in Israel would often go to search the Scriptures and to pray. The Garden of Gethsemane was among the places thus frequented. It was to this place, when the city of Jerusalem was hushed in the silence of midnight that Jesus often repaired for communion with His Father. When those to whom He had ministered all the day went every man to his house, Jesus, we read, "Went unto the Mount of Olives." He would sometimes take His disciples with Him to this place of retirement, that they might join their prayers with His. In prayer Christ had power with God, and He prevailed. Morning by morning, and evening by evening, He received grace that He might impart to others. Then, His soul replenished with grace and fervor, He would set forth to minister to the souls of men. (*Pastoral Ministry*, 282)

The five foolish virgins did not see the need to seek the oil daily. They were not willing to follow Christ's example set in the Mount of Olives, of spending time agonizing before God.

Those who are unwilling to deny self, to agonize before God, to pray long and earnestly for his blessing, will not obtain it. Wrestling with God—how few know what it is! How few have ever had their souls drawn out after God with intensity of desire until every power is on the stretch. When waves of despair which no language can express sweep over the suppliant, how few cling with unyielding faith to the promises of God. (*The Great Controversy*, 1888 ed., 621)

Just as Christ made the place of the olive his sanctuary for prayer, we too must be where the oil is found if we would be filled with that oil. Interestingly enough, Christ began to sweat as it were "great drops of blood" (Luke 22:44) right there in Gethsemane. Notice how Ellen White equates the blood with the oil.

"The blood drops of agony that from His wounded temples flowed down His face and beard were the pledge of His anointing with 'the oil of gladness' (Hebrews 1:9) as our great high priest" (*The Desire of Ages*, 734). Christ was being pressed for us to show us how we too may obtain the Spirit.

I saw how this grace could be obtained. Go to your closet and there alone plead with God. "'Create in me a clean heart, O God; and renew a right spirit within me'" Be in earnest, be sincere. Fervent prayer availeth much. In a Jacob-like manner, wrestle in prayer. Agonize. Jesus in the garden sweat great drops of blood; you must make an effort. Do not leave your closet until you feel strong in God; then watch, and just as long as you watch and pray, you can keep these evil besetments under, and the grace of God can, and will, appear in you. (*Amazing Grace*, 87)

Like the five wise virgins, we must have that oil *before* the crisis hits. Now is the time to be wise. We must have our own personal Gethsemane. In the garden, Peter, James, and John foolishly slept through this preparation time while Christ wisely prepared for the coming conflict (Mark 14:32–37). When the crisis hit, Christ was ready, calm, dignified. The disciples, however, were unprepared to the point of forsaking and even denying Christ. Let us learn the lesson. Drill now.

Group Discussion Questions

1. In what other ways can we see that our churches are in an oil crisis?

2. How can we, as individuals and as a church, find ways to go deeper in our experience with Christ?

3. Why is it important to store up on oil now, rather than wait for a crisis?

4. What are some of the causes for a lack of personal prayer time, and what can be done to move those things out of the way?

5. What from this chapter impacted you the most?

Chapter 2
Origin of the Oil Crisis

The first-ever experience of the wise and foolish being separated takes us back to the rebellion in heaven. Many lessons can be learned from the original oil crisis. It began when Lucifer (meaning "brightness" or "light-bearer") began to trust in his own light. Lucifer was known as the "anointed" cherub. The word "anointed" signifies that he was filled with the Spirit of God. In the Old Testament, everything in the sanctuary, including the covering cherubim, was anointed with oil signifying their holiness (see Exodus 40:9). Lucifer, the anointed cherub soon began to trust in his own light. "Thine heart was lifted up because of thy beauty, thou hast corrupted thy wisdom by reason of thy brightness" (Ezekiel 28:17).

Like the foolish virgins in Christ's parable whose wisdom was corrupted because they trusted in the light they had rather than in the Spirit behind that light, Lucifer corrupted his wisdom by trusting in his own righteousness. He neglected the "anointing" and instead focused on his "brightness." Soon, Lucifer was able to fill one-third of the angels in heaven with the same rebellious spirit, focusing on their light while rejecting the Spirit of God. The first shaking began to occur.

> Leaving his place in the immediate presence of God, Lucifer went forth to diffuse *the spirit* of discontent among the angels. Working with mysterious secrecy, and for a time concealing his real purpose under the appearance of reverence for God, he endeavored to excite dissatisfaction concerning the laws that governed heavenly beings, intimating that they imposed an unnecessary restraint. *Since their natures were holy*, he urged that the angels should obey the dictates of their own will. (*The Great Controversy*, 1888 ed., 495, emphasis added)

In the same way, the foolish virgins trusted in their own light, thus neglecting the Holy Spirit. Such a fatal mistake we would be wise to learn from.

Lucifer, the light-bearer, felt he could be like God without God's Spirit. In the book of Isaiah, he said, "I will ascend above the heights of the clouds; I will be like the most High" (Isaiah 14:14). In the Hebrew the word "clouds" is written in the singular, indicating that Lucifer said, "I will ascend *above the cloud.*" What cloud? When the children of Israel were in the desert, they were led by the presence of God in a cloud (see Exodus 13:21; 24:15, 16). The cloud was symbolic of God himself. Lucifer's desire to raise himself above *the cloud* was in essence attempting to raise himself above God.

His desire to ascend above the cloud denotes something else as well. The cloud was a symbol of prayer, communion with God, and intercession (see Leviticus 16:13; Revelation 8:3, 4). Lucifer was seeking to ascend without need of the cloud. He desired to ascend above God, bypassing the need to commune, or fellowship, with God. The foolish virgins made the same mistake. They desired to ascend when the bridegroom came and go into the wedding, which signifies the second coming, but without earnest communion with Christ. All who seek to "ascend" in this way, trusting in their own light while neglecting the anointing of God's Spirit, all who seek to ascend without need of the cloud or the oil, will share in Lucifer's fate. Though Lucifer sought to ascend, the Bible says of him, "Yet thou shalt be brought down to hell, to the sides of the pit" (Isaiah 14:15).

Lucifer did not go out alone. One-third of the heavenly angels were cast out with him (see Revelation 12:4–9). Here we find another major reason why the foolish virgins are lost in the end. They were infected and did not know it. When Lucifer sinned in heaven, he became infected with the deadly virus of sin. The Bible uses the illustration of leprosy to describe the dreadfulness of sin. Anyone who came into contact with a leper was himself contaminated with the disease.

Sin works in the same way, and the most effective way that Lucifer spread discontent in heaven was through the leprosy of slander and gossip. As each angel listened to the private arguments of Lucifer, little did they realize that they were being infected with Lucifer's leprosy. They were deceived by Lucifer's light, his appearance of righteousness. But his works contradicted the light he had. In the same way, the foolish virgins are deceived by false lights. They trust in themselves, and in their foolish companions.

Many, who are now gossiping, backbiting, giving ear to rumors, and speaking evil of their brothers and sisters, have been deceived into thinking that because they have light; they cannot possibly be lost. But their actions of unforgivingness, of hatred, and envy will seal their fate, as did Lucifer's. The worst thing was that the foolish virgins were blinded by their own light and did not realize their own danger.

The Wise Attend the School of Christ

The wise virgins, on the other hand, had learned not to look to their own light, but rather to depend upon the Spirit that gives light. The wise virgins were wise because they had been educated in the school of Christ. They learned that the work of the Holy Spirit was to make them more like Jesus, not merely outwardly but also inwardly. Like Jesus, the wise virgins understood the power of communion with God, for by it they obtained their wisdom. "It was in hours of solitary prayer that Jesus in His earth-life received *wisdom* and power." (*Child Guidance*, 525, emphasis added).

The five wise virgins spent solitary time in prayer. They attended the school of the Spirit and sat in the classroom of Christ. Every day the Holy Spirit has a roll-call marking who is in attendance in that day's class. The wise virgins are present while the foolish usually skip class. Of the foolish who do attend class, most, if not all, only stick around for roll-call and either disappear from class shortly afterward or have other things on their mind while the Teacher is speaking.

The wise understand the blessings of hard study and earnest prayer; they understand how important it is to know the Teacher personally. "Our prayers will take the form of a conversation with God as we would talk with a friend. He will speak His mysteries to us personally. Often there will come to us a sweet joyful sense of the presence of Jesus. Often our hearts will burn within us as He draws nigh to commune with us as He did with Enoch" (*Christ's Object Lessons*, 129). They can truly say, "I know Him!"

The wise study to be like Christ, and graduation occurs when they fully reflect His image and are then prepared to take their graduation pictures. "Christ is sitting for His portrait in every disciple" (*The Desire of Ages*, 826), "waiting with longing desire for the manifestation of Himself in His church. When the character of Christ shall be perfectly reproduced in His people, then He will come to claim them as His own" (*Christ's Object Lessons*, 69). What a day that will be when, at the graduation ceremony, the righteous stand upon the sea of glass mingled with fire and cast their graduation crowns at Jesus' feet.

The foolish, however, fail to realize that in the time of finals, they will be found sorely unprepared. Come the time of the finals, they will cry out, "give us your notes," or as the parable put it, "give us of your oil" (Matthew 25:8). But just as it is impossible to transfer what a wise man has learned over many years in the classroom to a foolish man who failed to consider the final exam, so the righteous are unable to help the foolish virgins in this parable. As Ellen White wrote:

> The class represented by the foolish virgins are not hypocrites. They have a regard for the truth, they have advocated the truth, they are attracted to those who believe the truth; but they have not yielded themselves to the Holy Spirit's working. ... They

have not studied His character; they have not *held communion with Him. ...*

They lull their hearts into security, and dream not of danger. When startled from their lethargy, they discern their destitution, and entreat others to supply their lack; but in spiritual things no man can make up another's deficiency. The grace of God has been freely offered to every soul. The message of the gospel has been heralded, "Let him that is athirst come. And whosoever will, let him take the water of life freely." Revelation 22:17. *But character is not transferable.* No man can believe for another. No man can receive the Spirit for another. No man can impart to another the character which is the fruit of the Spirit's working. ...

It is in a crisis that character is revealed. When the earnest voice proclaimed at midnight, "Behold, the bridegroom cometh; go ye out to meet him," and the sleeping virgins were roused from their slumbers, it was seen who had made preparation for the event. Both parties were taken unawares; but one was prepared for the emergency, and the other was found without preparation. (*Christ's Object Lessons*, 411, 412, emphasis added)

The preparation the wise made was in studying the character of Christ. This was the focus of the classroom sessions. Character is made up of thoughts and feelings. Therefore, to obtain the character of Christ is to obtain His thoughts and His feelings. By meditating upon Christ's life, His character (thoughts and feelings), and by beholding those thoughts and feelings, a mind transplant occurred where the wise, over time, assimilated Christ's character. So when the crisis came, when the time of trouble hit, the wise were able to respond with Christ's thoughts and His feelings and not their own. Just as Christ was calm and dignified when His captors took Him from Gethsemane, so the wise will reflect his peace in the storm. It is in this way that we receive the "mind of Christ" (see Philippians 2:5), thus, becoming wise and having the thought reflexes of Christ.

It would be well for us to spend a thoughtful hour each day in contemplation of the life of Christ. We should take it point by point, and let the imagination grasp each scene, especially the closing ones. As we thus dwell upon His great sacrifice for us, our confidence in Him will be more constant, our love will be quickened, and we shall be more deeply imbued with His spirit. (*The Desire of Ages*, 83)

The time is coming when oil will no longer be available. At that time, the foolish virgins will attempt to go "and buy" for themselves. While it is a noble effort to make up for lost time, the fact is that their time will have run out; probation will have closed. Christ will no longer be selling the oil. So who is in the parable? An imposter—one who looks like Jesus and sounds like Him but is, in fact, selling *foreign oil*. We would think that Seventh-day Adventists would know enough not to fall for Satan disguised as Jesus, but some will. Why? Their lamps will have gone out, and when a lamp goes out in the dark, it is impossible to see clearly.

Foolish Seventh-day Adventists who, at one time rejoiced in the light, will see Lucifer, the "light-bearer" as an "angel of light" (see 2 Corinthians 11:14). While they go to buy oil from the imposter, the bridegroom comes, which is the second coming. So when do the five foolish virgins get to speak to Christ asking Him to open the door to them since at the second coming the foolish die? It is not until the end of the millennium, when the foolish virgins come up in the *second resurrection*, that this conversation takes place. The foolish virgins realize from their study of Scripture that they have come up in the wrong resurrection. "Lord, Lord, open to us," they cry, "we don't belong out here with the wicked heathen." Christ's response will shock them. "Verily I say unto you, I know you not" (Matthew 25:12). How important it is to buy now while supplies last.

Group Discussion Questions

1. Why do you think Lucifer was successful in casting doubt in the minds of one-third of the angels about God's character?

2. How are leprosy and gossip alike? How do those infected with or by it become foolish?

3. In what ways can we begin to depend upon our own light while neglecting the oil?

4. Why is it unsafe to seek to buy the oil when it is too late?

5. What from this chapter impacted you the most?

Chapter 3
Oil Flow and the Dilemma of One Accord

The most formidable obstacle standing between the people of God and the final outpouring of the Holy Spirit is the issue of unity. Of Pentecost, the Bible records that "when the day of Pentecost was fully come, they were all with one accord in one place" (Acts 2:1). The disciples had their lamps burning brightly and were filled with the holy oil. One thing is evident from the responses of the wise and of the foolish virgins, both groups were perfectly united. "The foolish said unto the wise, Give us of your oil; for our lamps are gone out. But the wise answered, saying, Not so; lest there be not enough for us and you: but go ye rather to them that sell, and buy for yourselves" (Matthew 25:8, 9). Each group was perfectly united in their respective response, revealing that each group spoke as one person.

Ellen White described two groups of people in the time of the end; one group was bound "in bundles ready to burn," while the other group "seemed to be firmly united, and bound together by the truth, in bundles, or companies. Said the angel, 'The third angel is binding, or sealing, them in bundles for the heavenly garner'" (*Early Writings*, 88, 89). In the end, there will be only two groups of people—wise and foolish.

Our focus for this chapter is on the unity of the wise virgins. The wise virgins were united in their experience of receiving the outpouring of the heavenly oil, or the latter rain. The greatest threat to receiving this outpouring is division.

In the book of Acts, it is written that, they (120 people) were all of "one accord." As difficult as it may seem to get 120 people to come together in one accord, imagine the task at hand of assembling the millions of Seventh-day Adventists around the world to be in unity. To further complicate the issue, just consider some of the things that cause division in the church. There are such matters as music, conservatism versus liberalism, race, dress, Spirit of Prophecy, the nature of Christ, righteousness by faith. The list can go on and on. Will God's people ever be able to be of "one accord" so that the Spirit may be poured out? The answer is an encouraging "yes." But how?

In 1888, a message was given to this church through Elders Alonzo T. Jones and Elliot J. Waggoner that was calculated to bring God's people into unity. Ellen White said of it:

The Lord in His great mercy sent a most precious message to His people through Elders [E. J.] Waggoner and [A. T.] Jones. This message was to bring more prominently before the world the uplifted Saviour, the sacrifice for the sins of the whole world. It presented justification through faith in the Surety; it invited the people to receive the righteousness of Christ, which is made manifest in obedience to all the commandments of God. Many had lost sight of Jesus. (*Last Day Events*, 200)

Again she wrote, "The time of test is just upon us, for the loud cry of the third angel has already begun in the revelation of the righteousness of Christ, the sin-pardoning Redeemer. This is the beginning of the light of the angel whose glory shall fill the whole earth" (*Selected Messages*, Book 1, 362.

She summed it up well in these words, "Several have written to me, inquiring if the message of justification by faith is the third angel's message, and I have answered, 'It is the third angel's message in verity'" (*The Review and Herald*, April 1, 1890). "Justification by faith," "the righteousness of Christ, the sin-pardoning Redeemer,"—*this* is the message we are to receive and unite upon. What does this mean for us? What is justification anyway? How does the acceptance of this message enable us to receive the latter rain?

Justification means to be made right. And we are justified, or made right by the faith *of* Jesus, and faith *in* Jesus. The third angel's message ends with these words: "Here is the patience of the saints: here are they that keep the commandments of God, and the faith of Jesus" (Revelation 14:12).

The Faith *of* Jesus—what justifies us? Notice again:

Knowing that a man is not justified by the works of the law, but by the faith of Jesus Christ, even we have believed in Jesus Christ, that we might be justified by the faith of Christ, and not by the works of the law: for by the works of the law shall no flesh be justified. (Galatians 2:16, emphasis added)

How is it that Christ's faith justified us? The answer is profound. You see, faith looks upon present reality and sees something different than the natural eye. Faith sees the things that are not as though they were. Listen to how Jesus' faith justified us.

For when we were yet without strength, in due time Christ died for the ungodly. For scarcely for a righteous man will one die: yet peradventure for a good man some would even dare to die. But

God commendeth his love toward us, in that, while we were yet sinners, Christ died for us. Much more then, being now justified by his blood, we shall be saved from wrath through him. For if, when we were enemies, we were reconciled to God by the death of his Son, much more, being reconciled, we shall be saved by his life. (Romans 5:6–10)

When Jesus looked upon humanity, He saw a wretched sight. But by faith, He saw us for what we could be through Him. And He justified us, by His faith in what God could do in us. While we were His enemies, He justified us by His faith. Justified means "just-as-if-I'd" never sinned. While we were yet His enemies Christ extended to us justification. He saw us, just as if we'd never sinned. So how does this incredible truth help prepare us to receive God's Spirit?

When the wise virgins truly understood and received justification by the faith of Jesus, they were so awed at what He did for them, that they not only became recipients of His faith, but they also extended that same faith to others. They in turn saw others "just as if" they had never wronged them. (In contrast, see the parable of the wicked servant who was forgiven his debt, yet held account of others who owed him in Matthew 18:23–35.)

Is this not the great issue that currently keeps us divided? We are unwilling to forgive, unwilling to see each other as Christ saw us. If someone disagrees with us, we are ready to hate them with "godly hatred." We cannot pray with our brother or sister because they are not on the same page as us. We hold record of each other's sins and slights instead of forgiving regardless of having been asked.

If we truly understand this message of justification by faith as the verity of the third angel's message, we will cease to hold grudges against one another, and we will also cease "to justify" why we cannot pray together in a true spirit of unity. Ellen White wrote, "What is justification by faith? It is the work of God in laying the glory of man in the dust, and doing for man that which it is not in his power to do for himself. When men see their own nothingness, they are prepared to be clothed with the righteousness of Christ" (*The Faith I Live By*, 111).

Justification by faith, the third angel's message in verity, lays man's glory in the dust. How? By telling us that nothing we do, none of our works merit us to Christ. It is all His glory and none of ours. This lays our self-glorying in the dust. Isaiah experienced this kind of self realization when he cried, "Then said I, Woe is me! for I am undone; because I am a man of unclean lips, and I dwell in the midst of a people of unclean lips: for mine eyes have seen the King, the Lord of hosts" (Isaiah 6:5).

Commenting on this, Ellen White wrote:

> Isaiah had denounced the sin of others; but now he sees himself exposed to the same condemnation he had pronounced upon them. He had been satisfied with a cold, lifeless ceremony in his worship of God. He had not known this until the vision was given him of the Lord. How little now appeared his wisdom and talents as he looked upon the sacredness and majesty of the sanctuary. How unworthy he was! how unfitted for sacred service! His view of himself might be expressed in the language of the apostle Paul, "O wretched man that I am! who shall deliver me from the body of this death?" (*Seventh-day Adventist Bible Commentary*, 1139)

Have you ever noticed how it's the other people that are always presented as Laodicea? Everyone accuses everybody else as the cause of lukewarmness. When the third angel's message in verity, the faith of Jesus, is received, we will cease to point the finger at others and genuinely realize our own heart conditions. We will see ourselves as "wretched, and miserable, and poor, and blind, and naked" (Revelation 3:17). The "straight testimony" becomes applicable to us individually and personally.

"When men see their own nothingness, they are prepared to be clothed with the righteousness of Christ" (*The Faith I Live By*, 111). It is this nothingness upon which we must unite. We must unite upon the fact that we are all "wretched, and miserable, and poor, and blind, and naked." Our glory, our desire to be the greatest, even in righteous things, must be laid in the dust, and we must accept that we can be justified only as we realize our nothingness, and that Christ is our righteousness. We will then no longer compare ourselves among ourselves, for we will realize that we are all in the same boat—wretched and in need of the Holy Spirit. This is the unifying factor, our nothingness, and Christ's righteousness.

In the church today, many debates abound concerning the nature of Christ. One can get the answer to this question wrong and still be saved. However, there is a greater question; one we cannot get wrong and still be saved. That question is: *Which nature do I have?*

If it is not the one found in 2 Peter 1:4, we are indeed in trouble regardless of our theological stance on the human nature of Christ. "Whereby are given unto us exceeding great and precious promises: that by these ye might be partakers of the divine nature, having escaped the corruption that is in the world through lust" (2 Peter 1:4). We must become partakers of the divine nature of Christ. Without accepting this message, the third angel's message in verity, the wise virgins could never have expected to receive the rain. Only this could bring them into one accord. All their knowledge of truth availed nothing without the righteousness of Christ lived out in a practical manner.

The greatest deception of the human mind in Christ's day was that a mere assent to the truth constitutes righteousness. In all human experience a theoretical knowledge of the truth has been proved to be insufficient for the saving of the soul. It does not bring forth the fruits of righteousness. A jealous regard for what is termed theological truth often accompanies a hatred of genuine truth as made manifest in life. The darkest chapters of history are burdened with the record of crimes committed by bigoted religionists. The Pharisees claimed to be children of Abraham, and boasted of their possession of the oracles of God; yet these advantages did not preserve them from selfishness, malignity, greed for gain, and the basest hypocrisy. They thought themselves the greatest religionists of the world, but their so-called orthodoxy led them to crucify the Lord of glory.

The same danger still exists. Many take it for granted that they are Christians, simply because they subscribe to certain theological tenets. But they have not brought the truth into practical life. They have not believed and loved it; therefore, they have not received the power and grace that come through sanctification of the truth. Men may profess faith in the truth; but if it does not make them sincere, kind, patient, forbearing, heavenly minded, it is a curse to its possessors, and through their influence it is a curse to the world. (*The Desire of Ages*, 309)

The first disciples went forth preaching the word. They revealed Christ in their lives. And the Lord worked with them, "confirming the word with signs following." Mark 16:20. These disciples prepared themselves for their work. Before the day of Pentecost they met together, and put away all differences. They were of one accord. They believed Christ's promise that the blessing would be given, and they prayed in faith. (*The Desire of Ages*, 827)

Note that they did not debate all differences. Instead, they put them away. They knew that if they were Spirit-filled, all differences would take care of themselves; they would all be humbled enough to take rebuke, to learn, and to admit where mistakes had been made.

But there is more to this message of justification that must be accepted in order to be prepared for the latter rain. "Justification" means that there is an explainable cause for our actions. An understanding of justification as it relates to sin is the key to victory over sin. Justification is the state of being right with God. Again, Ellen White wrote, "The thought that the righteousness of Christ is imputed to us, not because of any merit on our part, but as a free gift from God, is a precious thought. The enemy of God and man is not willing that this truth should be clearly presented; for he knows that if the people receive it fully, his power will be broken" (*Gospel Workers*, 1892 ed., 103).

Justification by faith is so powerful a concept that to understand and experience it fully is to have the devil's power broken in our lives. How is this? We gain an incredible insight from the book *The Great Controversy*:

> It is impossible to so explain the origin of sin as to give a reason for its existence. Yet enough may be understood concerning both the origin and the final disposition of sin, to fully make manifest the justice and benevolence of God in all his dealings with evil. … Sin is an intruder, for whose presence no reason can be given. It is mysterious, unaccountable; to excuse it, is to defend it. Could excuse for it be found, or cause be shown for its existence, it would cease to be sin. (*The Great Controversy*, 1888 ed., 492)

In other words, there is no reason to sin. Think about that for a moment. Justification by faith pulls the cover off of every other type of justification. It tells us that man can be justified in no other way. It also shows that the only thing justifiable is that which is by faith. In other words, once we realize that there is no reason to sin, and live in accordance with that principle, we will cease to justify and do that for which we have no logical reason to do. In plain language, sin is illogical and stupid. It is like punching a wall because someone said hello to you. *Sin is not justifiable.*

Satan attempted to get Christ to justify sin in many ways. "Son of God, this is a good enough reason to retaliate against humanity, look how they are using you! This is good reason to turn stone into bread, for you are hungry. God has forsaken you; this is a good reason to come down from the cross." But none of these reasons made any logical sense to Jesus. They were in all actuality illogical to Him. So sin must become illogical to us before we start to behave like Jesus did. As it stands now, we justify why we are mad at others. There is a cause for my stealing, my lusting, my unhappiness, my covetousness, my retaliatory words. I looked *because* it was tempting. I fell *because* it was in my face. As long as we buy into the lie, that sin has *a cause;* we will continue to live by that lie.

Many of us use the fact that we are human to excuse sin. Will we, on the day of God, be able to use the fact that we were human as a justification for falling into sin? No! Every mouth will be stopped, and every reason will vanish as illogical when the whole guilty world stands before God without reason or explanation for their actions. They will then see how illogical sin was. Where there is no cause, there can be no effect. Jesus lived by this "no cause" principle. That is, He did that which was justifiable only by faith, and "faith cometh by hearing, and hearing by the Word of God" (Romans 10:17).

By accepting the third angel's message in verity, the wise virgins rid themselves of all self justification as to why they sin. By so doing, they effectively empty themselves and shift ideological paradigms, and receive the "mind of Christ," which sees sin as illogical. They, thus, cease to do that which to them has become illogical. This justification begins to be demonstrated in their lives on a daily basis. This is called sanctification. Sanctification is the unfolding result of justification by faith only.

When we go to the world with the loud cry, and point them to the broken law of God, the sincere will ask, "How then can man be justified?" We cannot point them to the law, which we have already done to make them aware of their guilt before God. We must point them to the solution for their guilt, the Lamb of God. No one will be justified (declared right) by the works of the law. Our mission will be to show the true meaning of justification.

So how can they be justified? First, they must cease to justify themselves in breaking God's law. They will see that they have "no logical reason," no justification for continuing to do so. Next, they will see that the only true justification is obtained by faith, which comes by hearing and that by the Word of God. They can only be justified by the things written in the Word accepted and lived out by the faith Christ had in God to work in and through us, thereby making us new creations! Then they too will cease to excuse sin and, having received the mind of Christ in seeing sin as illogical, will live accordingly by His divine nature in them. *This* is the message that is to lighten the earth with His glory!

The argument of perfection in the Seventh-day Adventist church has been a long-standing one. The truth is that *man cannot be perfect.* This is why Christ asks us to decrease, so that He may increase. When we decrease, when we lay our glory (pride) in the dust, then Christ becomes our glory, and He, the perfect One, lives out His perfection in us. The perfection is His, not ours. We are perfect when we cease to be, and Christ is all in all. We become perfect when we realize our own nothingness, step aside, cease to live justification by and of self, and begin to experience justification by the faith of Christ and in Christ.

That is perfection. We are incapable of it, but Christ in us is capable of it. Our work is not to seek perfection as much as it is to lay our glory in the dust so that the perfect Christ can live in and through us. He then becomes the perfect One, doing the perfect work. Christ in you, and in me, unifies us. Righteousness is no longer measured by what we do, but by what He does in and through us. It is measured by our nothingness. The more we decrease, the more He increases. When we experience this "nothingness," we will not exalt ourselves above one another for we will realize that we are nothing.

The message of justification by faith is calculated to stop us from seeking to justify ourselves in our attitudes of separation and hostility toward one another. It is calculated to put an end to the attitude of "who is the greatest" and a justification of why we sin. Will we accept this message? Will we lay our glory in the dust and seek Christ at the foot of the cross?

When we unite on this point, the Spirit will be poured out, and that on which we had not yet seen eye to eye will be made plain. Because our hearts have been softened, we will be ready and willing to receive correction. If we accept our nothingness and unite on that, pleading to God in our utter helplessness, He will hear. We will be of one accord, though scattered around the world in many places.

We must not wait for the day when we, by our own efforts, cause others to see all things in the same way we do before we come together to pray. That day will never come. May God help all—the liberal, the conservative, the black, the white, the Asian, the Latino, the leader, and the layman—to realize and unite upon our nothingness, and Christ's righteousness.

In 1888 there was much debate, much bitterness, and much separation over the message of justification by faith and Christ our righteousness. We now have an opportunity again to come together, humble ourselves, and unite upon the righteousness of Christ and our own nothingness. We are at a crossroads. Again, the decision is ours. Will we pass the test?

Group Discussion Questions

1. What is justification by faith?
2. Does unity equal compromise?
3. What do you think keeps us from coming together at the foot of the cross?
4. Why do we withhold justification by faith from others?
5. What from this chapter affected you most?

Chapter 4
Amazing Grace and the Loud Cry

L et's start with a question: Is there anything for which you would consider worth suffering the second death? Is there anything for which you would trade your place in heaven? If you answered "no," like many Seventh-day Adventists have, there is a big problem. This problem explains why the latter rain cannot yet fall upon God's people. We'll come back to this question later in this chapter.

In the oriental arts, there is something known as *Dim Mak*, or the death touch. A martial artist, who has studied this art, it is supposed, can hit a person at a specific point on the body, causing that person to expire in a matter of hours to days. Though he may walk away alive from the fight, the person is as good as dead. Though this is a definite form of spiritualism, it is also a counterfeit of the genuine death touch delivered at Calvary 2,000 years ago. Jesus died on a hill called "Calvary." The Greek is *kranion*, from which we get our English word "cranium." Matthew 27:33 calls it "Golgotha, that is to say, a place of the skull." In fulfillment of the prophecy of Genesis 3:15, Jesus, the Seed, delivered a "bruise," or death touch, to Satan. Though he walked away alive from the showdown at Calvary, Satan is as good as dead.

At the cross we too received a death touch. Our carnal minds must be bruised, broken, and put to death. God's people must be as good as dead to self in order to receive the latter rain, and this death can happen only as our minds focus upon the cross of Christ. Self must receive the death touch.

In fact, the latter rain, the outpouring of the Holy Spirit, is a special outpouring of the spirit of *self-sacrifice* upon the people of God. The Bible calls it the "spirit of grace." "I will pour upon the house of David, and upon the inhabitants of Jerusalem, the *spirit of grace* and of supplications" (Zechariah 12:10, emphasis added). This is the spirit that the five wise virgins possessed.

Notice that Ellen White also mentioned this "spirit of grace."

But near the close of earth's harvest, a special bestowal of *spiritual grace* is promised to prepare the church for the coming of the Son of man. (*The Acts of the Apostles*, 55, emphasis added).

We must seek His favors with the whole heart if the *showers of grace* are to come to us. (*The Faith I Live By*, 334, emphasis added).

Let us, with contrite hearts, pray most earnestly that now, in the time of the latter rain, the *showers of grace* may fall upon us. (*Testimonies to Ministers and Gospel Workers*, 508, emphasis added).

We must not wait for the latter rain. It is coming upon all who will recognize and appropriate the dew and *showers of grace* that fall upon us. ... The whole earth is to be filled with the glory of God. (*Manuscript Releases*, vol. 2, 18, emphasis added)

So what is grace? Grace is defined as a favorable act. It is the way God saves us.

God might have sent His Son into the world to condemn the world. But amazing grace! Christ came to save, not to destroy. (*Mind, Character, and Personality*, 249)

Grace is the way that Jesus saves: "Being justified freely by his grace" (Romans 3:24).

It is at the cross that this grace, amazing grace, was demonstrated. Hence, as Christians experiencing this grace, we must extend this grace to others. We must love one another as Christ loved us with such amazing grace. But how many of us actually love one another? Do you love the person in the church you least know?

Ellen White told us:

The message of the renewing power of God's grace will be carried to every country and clime, until the truth shall belt the world. (*Counsels to Parents, Teachers, and Students*, 532)

When the five wise virgins trimmed their lamps, their fire was "renewed." (We will discuss this in more depth in the following chapter.) In this action they experienced "the renewing power of God's grace," and it this message that lightens the world.

However, the reason that the three angels' messages have not been accompanied by the outpouring of grace is because we have not yet experienced that "renewing power" of grace. Therefore, we are not yet able to extend it to one another, and ultimately to the world.

When the latter rain is poured out, the church will be clothed with power for its work; but the church as a whole will never receive this until its members shall put away from among them, envy, evil-surmisings, and evil-speaking. Those who cherish these sins know not the blessed experience of love; they are not awake to the fact that the Lord is testing and proving their love for him *by the attitude they assume toward one another.* (*The Review and Herald*, October 6, 1896, emphasis added)

Grace is how God forgave us, by sending His Son to die for us. Therefore, a special spirit of forgiveness is to pervade the church in an overflowing flood. "Forbearing one another, and forgiving one another, if any man have a quarrel against any: even as Christ forgave you, so also do ye" (Colossians 3:13).

To forgive as Christ forgave, we must understand how He forgave. We gain insight into the depth of Christ's forgiveness in the book of Isaiah. Said the prophet:

- Isaiah 53:3—He is despised and rejected of men; a man of sorrows, and acquainted with grief: and we hid as it were our faces from him; he was despised, and we esteemed him not.

- Isaiah 53:4—Surely he hath borne our griefs, and carried our sorrows: yet we did esteem him stricken, smitten of God, and afflicted.

- Isaiah 53:5—But he was wounded for our transgressions, he was bruised for our iniquities: the chastisement of our peace was upon him; and with his stripes we are healed.

- Isaiah 53:6—All we like sheep have gone astray; we have turned every one to his own way; and the Lord hath laid on him the iniquity of us all.

These verses reveal Christ as a man of sorrows, not because of His own suffering, but because He bore "our griefs, and carried our sorrows." The word "borne" in Isaiah 53:4 means to carry, to bear, to forgive. Amazing grace! Christ became so identified with us that He took our sin upon Himself as if they were His own. This is forgiveness! It is identifying with the one who wronged you so much that you take their sin upon yourself and carry that sin on his or her behalf to God as if it were your own!

Remember when Israel had sinned against God, and Moses went up into the mount to seek forgiveness for them? Moses, who reflected the image of Christ, pleaded with God to put their sin to his account! "Moses returned unto the Lord, and said, Oh, this people have sinned a great sin, and have made them gods of gold. Yet now, if thou wilt forgive their sin—; and if not, blot me, I pray thee, out of thy book which thou hast written" (Exodus 32:31, 32). Amazing grace!

Christ on the cross prayed for our forgiveness and demonstrated that this was to go beyond mere words. Instead, He actually took those sins upon 'Himself and presented them to God the Father as though they were His own. When we learn to forgive like Jesus forgave, the Spirit "of grace and of supplication" will surely fall. But sadly, as an alternative, many pray or wish the worst for their enemies.

True forgiveness is the offer to let one go of the demand of justice while you yourself suffer the loss. Forgiveness is acquittal. We cannot receive the latter rain until we acquit one another. Only those who acquit will receive the spirit. The three angels' messages are powerless in demonstration unless we have this amazing grace. Our enemies must become to us as spiritual paralytics. We must take their sins against us to Jesus pleading for their forgiveness as though they could not do it themselves, pleading for those sins with an urgency as though they were our own.

Instead, many of us demand justice. We demand to be recompensed by the one who has wronged us. But in demanding justice without mercy, we condemn ourselves by the same standard. No man will be saved by justice, but by mercy. When we seek mercy for not only ourselves but for others, we receive the same from God. He is the just One, the only One who can demand justice without it being suicidal.

The lost experience justice; the saved receive mercy. If we do not forgive (extend grace), we will not be forgiven (see Matthew 6:15). Sin demands that the other take the loss, forgiveness is the taking of the loss upon one's self, forfeiting the demand for justice.

In fact, God's view of perfection is the taking of another's sins upon one's self while innocent in exchange for the forgiveness of that same person, identifying with the sin of the one who has wronged us as if it were our own. In taking the very sin against us upon us, we free them to be forgiven by God if they will accept it, and we free ourselves from the condemnation of demanding justice upon our enemies.

> Ye have heard that it hath been said, Thou shalt love thy neighbour, and hate thine enemy. But I say unto you, Love your enemies, bless them that curse you, do good to them that hate you, and pray for them which despitefully use you, and persecute you; that ye may be the children of your Father which is in heaven:

for he maketh his sun to rise on the evil and on the good, and sendeth rain on the just and on the unjust. For if ye love them which love you, what reward have ye? do not even the publicans the same? And if ye salute your brethren only, what do ye more than others? do not even the publicans so? Be ye therefore perfect, even as your Father which is in heaven is perfect. (Matthew 5:43–48)

"If he is lost, let it not be on account of his sin against me," must be our prayer for those who have wronged us. This kind of earnest prayer is only possible for a man who has died to self. The cross delivers the touch of grace that destroys the carnal mind. The greatest evidence of a spiritually dead man is his willingness to forgive his enemy. Grace requires that I die to self that my enemy might live. I yield the right to be vindicated, so that my antagonist might live. "Greater love hath no man than this, that a man lay down his life for his friends" (John 15:13).

Galatians 6:1, 2 tells us to "bear one another's burdens" (weights) and so fulfill the law of Christ. In other words, we fulfill the law when we love one another so much that we are willing, like Moses, to give to Christ the burdens that others commit against us. This is true love, potent love.

Amazing grace goes even deeper than this. Jesus was willing to die, quite literally, to save us. True love, true grace demands that we be willing to die, to lay down our lives for the brethren. For this reason Christ says, "A new commandment I give unto you, that ye love one another; as I have loved you, that ye also love one another" (John 13:34).

How did Jesus love us? Paul wrote, "I am crucified with Christ: nevertheless I live; yet not I, but Christ liveth in me: and the life which I now live in the flesh I live by the faith of the Son of God, who loved me, and gave himself for me" (Galatians 2:20). Christ demonstrated that true grace is the willingness to lay down our lives for another, to give ourselves for others. Until God's people get to the place that, like the early church, we are willing to lay down our lives for the sake of the gospel, and our brethren, we cannot expect to experience the power of the early church.

Jesus did not die just for His friends. "But God commendeth his love toward us, in that, while we were yet sinners, Christ died for us" (Romans 5:8). Hence, we must be willing to lay down our lives even for our enemies, the very ones we've been struggling to forgive. We must love not our lives "unto the death" (see Revelation 12:11).

Christ's amazing grace is even more amazing than this. Back to our question at the beginning of the chapter: Is there any reason for which you would be willing to suffer the second death? Your answer should be yes.

Notice the following quote:

> Three times has He uttered that prayer. Three times has humanity shrunk from the last, crowning sacrifice. But now the history of the human race comes up before the world's Redeemer. He sees that the transgressors of the law, if left to themselves, must perish. He sees the helplessness of man. He sees the power of sin. The woes and lamentations of a doomed world rise before Him. He beholds its impending fate, and His decision is made. He will save man *at any cost to Himself.* (*The Desire of Ages,* 690, emphasis added)

What did that "any cost" include?

> Satan with his fierce temptations wrung the heart of Jesus. The Saviour could not see through the portals of the tomb. Hope did not present to Him His coming forth from the grave a conqueror, or tell Him of the Father's acceptance of the sacrifice. He feared that sin was so offensive to God that Their separation was to be eternal. (*The Desire of Ages,* 753)

Jesus loved us so much, He was willing to suffer the second death, rather than desert us or save Himself at our expense. Jesus was willing to be blotted out. In fact, when Moses prayed, "blot me ... out of thy book," He was actually praying to experience the second death. He was willing to miss out on heaven itself, rather than see God's rebellious people lost.

We must be willing to die the second death, *while remaining faithful to God,* not only for our friend but also for our enemy. Not that God will honor the request, but in so doing we exemplify the character of Christ. This is the amazing grace we must experience before we can go out to the world in fullness of His power. It is impossible to hate someone for whom you are willing to die the second death. This is ultimate love. Moved by this love, God's church will have power unparalleled.

This may come as a shock, but our ultimate goal is not heaven, but rather to reflect the character of Christ. Remember, Satan also desires, perhaps more than many of us, to go to heaven (see Isaiah 14:12–14). Jesus' ultimate goal was not heaven but the saving of others!

On Christ's life, Ellen White wrote:

> Jesus did not count heaven a place to be desired while we were lost. He left the heavenly courts for a life of reproach and insult, and a death of shame. He who was rich in heaven's priceless

treasure, became poor, that through His poverty we might be rich. We are to follow in the path He trod.

Love for souls for whom Christ died means crucifixion of self. He who is a child of God should henceforth look upon himself as a link in the chain let down to save the world, one with Christ in His plan of mercy, going forth with Him to seek and save the lost. The Christian is ever to realize that he has consecrated himself to God, and that in character he is to reveal Christ to the world. The self-sacrifice, the sympathy, the love, manifested in the life of Christ are to reappear in the life of the worker for God. (*The Desire of Ages*, 416, 417)

Jesus said, "If any man will come after me, let him deny himself, and take up his cross, and follow me. For whosoever will save his life shall lose it: and whosoever will lose his life for my sake shall find it" (Matthew 16:24, 25). The person who puts heaven as his ultimate goal has missed the point. Self sacrifice must extend even to the second death. When the crisis hits, Satan will accuse the people of God of serving Him out of the fear of hell or for reward of heaven, but this is not the case; it is because they love Him. In response, God's Spirit will be withdrawn, leaving the righteous to wonder if they have been forsaken by God. Like Christ on the cross, they will wonder if God has forsaken them.

As Satan accuses the people of God on account of their sins, the Lord permits him to try them to the uttermost. Their confidence in God, their faith and firmness, will be severely tested. As they review the past, their hopes sink; for in their whole lives they can see little good. They are fully conscious of their weakness and unworthiness. Satan endeavors to terrify them with the thought that their cases are hopeless, that the stain of their defilement will never be washed away. He hopes so to destroy their faith that they will yield to his temptations and turn from their allegiance to God.

Though God's people will be surrounded by enemies who are bent upon their destruction, yet the anguish which they suffer is not a dread of persecution for the truth's sake; they fear that every sin has not been repented of, and that through some fault in themselves they will fail to realize the fulfillment of the Saviour's promise: I "will keep thee from the hour of temptation, which shall come upon all the world." Revelation 3:10. If they could have the assurance of pardon they would not shrink from torture or death; but should they prove unworthy, and lose their lives because of their own defects of character, then God's holy name would be reproached. (*The Great Controversy*, 619)

Their main concern will be God's name. When Satan tempts them with the thought that they have been forsaken by God and might as well sin, like Job, they will respond, "Though he slay me, yet will I trust in him: but I will maintain mine own ways before him" (Job 13:15).

Heaven will be populated by people who loved Christ so much that they were willing to forsake even heaven for Him! When a person has experienced the kind of grace, amazing grace that extends even unto the second death, the devil has no more power over him.

Forasmuch then as the children are partakers of flesh and blood, he also himself likewise took part of the same; that through death he might destroy him that had the power of death, that is, the devil; and deliver them who through fear of death were all their lifetime subject to bondage. (Hebrews 2:14, 15)

It is the fear of death that keeps us in bondage. Once this fear is cast off by a love stronger than even the second death, the devil has no more power or dominion over us. It is "through death" that we gain power over Satan.

Herein is our love made perfect, that we may have boldness in the day of judgment: because as he is, so are we in this world. There is no fear in love; but perfect love casteth out fear: because fear hath torment. He that feareth is not made perfect in love. (1 John 4:17, 18)

For he that is dead is freed from sin. (Romans 6:7)

Again, we must receive this death touch at Calvary. The problem with God's people is that we are having too many "near-death" experiences. We must die and experience the death touch daily, as did Paul (see Galatians 2:20).

We would then rather die than sin, rather die than hold a grudge, rather be blotted out than sit idly by refusing to witness to lost souls, and we would then indeed be filled with the Spirit. We will be moved to witness to the world "at any cost" to ourselves. This is the fiery boldness possessed by the five virgins.

When the storm of persecution really breaks upon us, the true sheep will hear the true Shepherd's voice. *Self-denying* efforts will be put forth to save the lost, and many who have strayed from the fold will come back to follow the great Shepherd. (*Testimonies for the Church*, vol. 6, 400, emphasis added)

To every soul that accepts Jesus, the cross of Calvary speaks: "Behold the worth of the soul: 'Go ye into all the world, and preach the gospel to every creature.'" Nothing is to be permitted to hinder this work. It is the all-important work for time; it is to be far-reaching as eternity. *The love that Jesus manifested* for the souls of men in the sacrifice which He made for their redemption, *will actuate all His followers.* (*Testimonies for the Church*, 455, emphasis added)

This is when the world will know that we are His disciples. "By this shall all men know that ye are my disciples, if ye have love one to another" (John 13:35). This transformation literally confounds Satan.

The Lord Jesus is making experiments on human hearts through the exhibition of His mercy and abundant grace. He is effecting transformations so amazing that Satan, with all his triumphant boasting, with all his confederacy of evil united against God and the laws of His government, stands viewing them as a fortress impregnable to his sophistries and delusions. They are to him an incomprehensible mystery. (*Testimonies to Ministers and Gospel Workers*, 208)

Group Discussion Questions

1. What impacted you most from this chapter?
2. How do you view the grace of God from what you have read?
3. How can we obtain and exercise that same grace?
4. Why is it so hard to extend that grace to our enemies?
5. Discuss the concept of willingness to give up all for heaven, even heaven itself.

Chapter 5
Where There Is No Wood

The five foolish virgins had a major problem. They ran out of oil. One of the most pressing questions of this parable is the question of just how they came to run out of oil. The book of Proverbs, a book of wisdom, lays out a very simple principle that has a profound impact upon this parable. Proverbs 26:20, 21 reads, "Where no wood is, there the fire goeth out: so where there is no talebearer, the strife ceaseth. As coals are to burning coals, and wood to fire; so is a contentious man to kindle strife." The principles in these two verses are common sense. Where there is no wood, no fuel, the fire must, and eventually will, go out.

Wood is a source of fuel. In fact, this point is perhaps the most overlooked, yet the most crucial part of this parable. Bible students usually compare the passage found in Zechariah, chapter 4, to answer the meaning of the oil and the lamp in the parable of ten virgins in Matthew 25. Yet a comparison of the two portions of scripture reveals something vital. Here is the passage again:

> The angel that talked with me came again, and waked me, as a man that is wakened out of his sleep, And said unto me, What seest thou? And I said, I have looked, and behold a candlestick all of gold, with a bowl upon the top of it, and his seven lamps thereon, and seven pipes to the seven lamps, which are upon the top thereof: And two olive trees by it, one upon the right side of the bowl, and the other upon the left side thereof. So I answered and spake to the angel that talked with me, saying, What are these, my lord? Then the angel that talked with me answered and said unto me, Knowest thou not what these be? And I said, No, my lord. Then he answered and spake unto me, saying, This is the word of the Lord unto Zerubbabel, saying, Not by might, nor by power, but by my spirit, saith the Lord of hosts. (Zechariah 4:1–6)

Notice that the oil comes from trees—wood. But what do these two trees represent? The angel in Zechariah continued:

> Then answered I, and said unto him, What are these two olive trees upon the right side of the candlestick and upon the left

side thereof? And I answered again, and said unto him, What be these two olive branches which through the two golden pipes empty the golden oil out of themselves? And he answered me and said, Knowest thou not what these be? And I said, No, my lord. Then said he, These are the two anointed ones, that stand by the Lord of the whole earth. (Zechariah 4:11–14)

"The two anointed ones that stand by," or beside "the Lord of the whole earth" (*The Review and Herald*, July 20, 1897) represent the covering cherubim who stood closest in the presence of God (see Exodus 25:17–22). "The anointed ones standing by the Lord of the whole earth, have the position once given to Satan as covering cherub. By the holy beings surrounding his throne, the Lord keeps up a constant communication with the inhabitants of the earth" (*The Review and Herald*, July 20, 1897).

These two anointed ones, who stand closest to the presence of God the Father, Son, and Holy Spirit, have the greatest insight into the mysteries of the plan of redemption, just as Lucifer once did, in holding that position. "He [Lucifer] had been the highest of all created beings, and had been foremost in revealing God's purposes to the universe" (*The Desire of Ages*, 758).

These angels, having taken Lucifer's place, now bear the responsibility of pointing men to the mystery of salvation. "The mission of the two anointed ones is to communicate to God's people that heavenly grace which alone can make His word a lamp to the feet and a light to the path. 'Not by might, nor by power, but by My Spirit, saith the Lord of hosts.' Zechariah 4:6" (*Christ's Object Lessons*, 408).

The work of the angel in this vision is to point us to the plan of redemption. But how? Notice, that both appear, not as angels, *but each as a tree*. Why would the angels commissioned to "communicate that heavenly grace" appear as a tree? Could it be that they were trying to direct our minds to the tree of Calvary? Have we missed this point? *The oil came from the tree.* Where there is no wood, the fire goes out. Where there is not a cross, there can be no fire.

In fact, if we look closer at the vision of Zechariah, there are *three* trees—the two olive trees and the *seven-branched* candlestick. That's right, the seven branched candlestick was actually a tree. This is why Exodus 25:31–33 describes it as having "buds," "flowers," "almonds," and "knops." Yes, three trees to remind us of the scene at Calvary where three trees reveal that Christ died for the righteous and the wicked alike—three trees centering around the plan of redemption. In fact, I believe the following statements can only truly be understood, when we realize that

Calvary's Tree is the place upon which Christ, "the light of the world" brought glory to His Father in heaven.

> Neither do men light a candle, and put it under a bushel, *but on a candlestick; and it giveth light unto all that are in the house.* Let your light so shine before men, that they may see your good works, and glorify your Father which is in heaven. (Matthew 5:15, emphasis added)

> *In the light from Calvary* it will be seen that the law of self-re-nouncing love is the law of life for earth and heaven; that the love which "seeketh not her own" has its source in the heart of God; and that in the meek and lowly One is manifested the character of Him who dwelleth in the light which no man can approach unto. (*The Desire of Ages*, 19, emphasis added)

> Since the Saviour shed His blood for the remission of sins, and ascended to heaven "to appear in the presence of God for us" (Hebrews 9:24), *light has been streaming from the cross of Calvary* and from the holy places of the sanctuary above. (*Patriarchs and Prophets*, 367, emphasis added)

> It is our privilege also to glory in the cross, our privilege to give ourselves wholly to Him who gave Himself for us. Then, *with the light that streams from Calvary shining in our faces*, we may go forth to reveal this light to those in darkness. (*The Acts of the Apostles*, 210, emphasis added)

Yes, where there is no wood, where the cross is neglected, or its principles rejected, there can be no oil. Where there is no oil, no Holy Spirit, the fire will go out. This reveals something amazing about the five foolish virgins. They had the light of the cross, they understood the sacrifice of Christ, and mentally accepted it, but they did not possess the spirit behind the cross, the spirit of "self-sacrificing love" displayed at the cross.

They lost the spirit of sacrifice. In their early days, they would have sacrificed anything to make it to prayer meeting, to Sabbath School. Wherever God's presence was, there they wanted to be. Their money and their time was not their own because it belonged to God. Over time they began to lose that fire, that burning desire to serve God. The fire was no longer greater than their likes and dislikes, pet peeves, and pet sins.

Slowly, they lost their first love; they became lukewarm—no longer hot and not really cold either. They lost the anointing oil that would have enlightened their eyes to see in the darkness. They ignored Christ's counsel: "I counsel thee to buy of me gold tried in the fire, that thou mayest be rich; and white raiment, that thou mayest be clothed, and that the shame of thy nakedness do not appear; *and anoint thine eyes with eyesalve, that thou mayest see*" (Revelation 3:18, emphasis added). The Greek word for anoint in this verse is *egchrio*: to rub in (oil), besmear, anoint. Their lamps went out, and they became "blind."

The solution then to our fire not going out is a very simple one. Get more wood. Get more of the cross. This is why Jesus said, "If any man will come after me, let him deny himself, and take up his cross, and follow me" (Matthew 16:24).

> *Be not like the foolish virgins, who take for granted that the promises of God are theirs, while they do not follow the injunctions of Christ.* Christ teaches us that profession is nothing. "If any man will come after me," He says, "let him deny himself, and take up his cross daily, and follow me." (*Maranatha*, 54, emphasis added)

The more we focus on the cross, the greater the fire of God's love burns within our hearts. The more we turn away from living by the principles of the cross, the principles of self-sacrificing love, the sooner the fire begins to die. More wood, more fire. No wood, no fire.

This parable shows that when the crisis hit, the five foolish asked for the oil of the five wise. "But the wise answered, saying, Not so; lest there be not enough for us and you: but go ye rather to them that sell, and buy for yourselves" (Matthew 25:9). "Them that sell," is a reference to the two anointed ones from which the oil is dispersed into the tree-lamp. Remember these two anointed ones stand in the presence of God, in particular "above the mercy seat."

The five foolish were encouraged to go before the throne of grace, of which it is written, "Let us therefore come boldly unto the throne of grace, that we may obtain *mercy*, and find grace to help in time of need" (Hebrews 4:16, emphasis added). The five foolish virgins' "time of need" was too late.

The ten virgins all appear to understand that the oil was being sold, that it had to be bought. In order to buy the oil, each one needed to have something to give in exchange. But what can one give in order to gain the Holy Spirit? *Sin*. God has a "Sins for Oil" program.

According to the apostle Peter, it works this way. "Repent, and be baptized every one of you in the name of Jesus Christ for the remission of sins, and ye shall receive the gift of the Holy Ghost" (Acts 2:38). Through repentance, that is confessing, giving our sins to God, and turning from our wicked ways, He trades with us His Spirit. God says "Give me your 'self,' and I will give you My 'Self.' Give me your sins, and I will give you my Spirit."

> It is his Holy Spirit that impresses us with the necessity of empty-ing the soul of all selfishness; and when we give ourselves to God, *he will fill the vacuum with his divine Spirit*, and give us the pre-cious graces of his own character. (*The Bible Echo*, July 1, 1892, emphasis added)

This "Sins for Oil" program was what filled the five wise virgins' lamps with oil. At the cross, the lamp-tree, they saw the goodness of God, and "the goodness of God" led them to "repentance" (Romans 2:4), and they repented, giving their sins to Him and receiving the Holy Ghost in exchange. Since then, any sin brought to their attention, they took to God, confessed it, turned from it, and in return, God commissioned that more oil flow through Calvary, causing their fire to burn brighter. The moment we cease to repent, the moment we begin to hide sin in our hearts, the moment we are content to hold on to secret sin, the moment we neglect to make right the wrongs we alone know we have done to oth-ers—that is the moment the Spirit ceases to flow. Light is there, and one may trust in that light, but it is merely a flicker. We have separated our-selves from the Tree through which the oil flows. The greatest deception is to trust in light while not realizing that its source has been cut off. This deception kept the foolish virgins trusting in their own light.

The five foolish virgins at some point had dropped out of the "Sins for Oil" program. They began to hold on to sin, bitterness, hidden agendas, secret sins, and failed to forgive. In so doing, in no longer being moved by the goodness of God demonstrated at the tree of Calvary, in rejecting the spirit which flows through the cross, while theoretically acknowledging the light of the cross, they eventually cut themselves from the oil, and the light eventually goes out.

So in their time of need, the five foolish virgins go to the throne of grace to confess their sins, only to find that the "Sins for Oil" program has ended. Probation has closed. The anointed ones have ceased their work of dispensing oil. "*Now is probationary time*, before the angel shall fold her golden wings, the *angel of mercy, and shall step down from the throne, and mercy, mercy is gone forever*" (*Seventh-day Adventist Bible Commentary*, 989, emphasis added).

Now is probationary time. Be wise. Gather the wood. More wood, more fire. "Where no wood is, there the fire goeth out."

Group Discussion Questions

1. What impacted you the most about this chapter?
2. Discuss the concept of having more "wood."
3. What was the mistake of the five foolish virgins?
4. Why is it important to confess and make right with others known wrongs?
5. Why is it foolish to wait to repent?
6. In what ways can we tell personally when the fire is going out?
7. In what ways can we feed the fire so that it does not go out?

Chapter 6
Lighten Up

Another unspoken, but crucial, aspect of the parable of the ten virgins is the wick of the lamp. "At midnight there was a cry made, Behold, the bridegroom cometh; go ye out to meet him. Then all those virgins arose, and trimmed their lamps" (Matthew 25:6, 7). The trimming of the lamps indicated that these lamps had wicks. In the Old Testament, "snuffers" where used in the sanctuary to trim the wicks of the candlestick (see Exodus 37:23).

So what would the wicks symbolize? In the candle-making business, the wick is known as "the heart of the candle." Without your heart, God has nothing to work with. Where there is no wick, there can be no fire.

The trimming of the wick served three purposes. First, the candle would burn brighter. Second, the candle would burn longer. Third, the candle would burn cleaner. An improperly trimmed wick leads to a black, ashy, smoky substance called "soot." Hence, when the five wise virgins trimmed their lamps, it caused their fire to "lighten up," to burn brighter, longer, and cleaner. However, when the five foolish attempted to trim theirs, they discovered the soot of sin had blackened their candlesticks and their hearts.

The issue for those who would be wise virgins is very simple. *Lighten up!* Burn brighter. According to the Old Testament, the wicks were to be trimmed every morning or evening.

> Command the children of Israel, that they bring unto thee pure oil olive beaten for the light, to cause the lamps to burn continually. Without the vail of the testimony, in the tabernacle of the congregation, shall Aaron order it from the evening unto the morning before the Lord continually: it shall be a statute for ever in your generations. He shall order the lamps upon the pure candlestick before the Lord continually. (Leviticus 24:2–4)

Commenting on Leviticus 24:4, the Jamieson, Fausset, Brown Commentary[2] says, "The daily presence of the priests was necessary to

---

2   Robert Jamieson, A. R. Fausset, and David Brown, *Commentary Critical and Explanatory on the Whole Bible* (Hartford, Connecticut: S. S. Scranton and Company, 1871), accessed from e-Sword software, version 10.1.0.

superintend the cleaning and trimming." In other words, the wicks were to be kept freshly trimmed. In trimming the lamps, excess is being removed. This is work we must do correctly so that our lights will not burn out. The excess of bitterness, malice, envy, evil surmising, gossip, lack of forgiveness, and hatred must all be cut off. The excess of the pleasures of this world, its music, its fashions, and its entertainment must be eliminated from the *wick of the heart*, lest we be found with *a wicked heart*.

Another lesson of vital importance is that we cannot depend on yesterday's or yesteryear's fires. We cannot depend on our old experiences to keep us burning. We must be having a daily, fresh, and new experience with Christ. So how do we effectively trim the wick to burn more brightly, to "lighten up"? There are five ways to trim the excesses of sin from the heart.

- **Bible Study**

  By studying the Word of God or becoming more efficient in the study of God's Word, we are trimming the excess. We should study the undiluted three angels' messages in its full power. We should remove all frills from the message to teach and preach it as very straight testimony. The more we study the Word of God, the more "heartburn" we shall receive. *Bible study helps us to lighten up.*

  The five foolish virgins in neglecting a study of God's Word, waited for a time until it was too late to be benefited by His Word. "They shall wander from sea to sea, and from the north even to the east, they shall run to and fro to seek the word of the Lord, and shall not find it" (Amos 8:12).

- **Prayer**

  Prayer is also vital for those who wish to "lighten up." Prayer is the breath of the soul, and we know that without oxygen, fire dies. The disciples prayed for ten days, and in answer to their earnest prayer, the oil of God's spirit fell from heaven and lit their lamps. "Suddenly there came a sound from heaven as of a rushing mighty wind [*pnoē* in the Greek means respiration, a breeze, breath, wind[3]] and it filled all the house where they were sitting. And there appeared unto them cloven tongues like as of fire, and it sat upon each of them" (Acts 2:2, 3). *Prayer helps us to lighten up.* The five foolish virgins, in neglecting to commune with God, sought to commune with Him in a time when He did not answer.

> Because I have called, and ye refused; I have stretched out my hand, and no man regarded; But ye have set at nought all my

---

3   James Strong, *Strong's Exhaustive Concordance of the Bible* (New York: Abingdon Press, 1890), accessed from e-Sword software, version 10.1.0.

counsel, and would none of my reproof: I also will laugh at your calamity; I will mock when your fear cometh; When your fear cometh as desolation, and your destruction cometh as a whirlwind; when distress and anguish cometh upon you. Then shall they call upon me, but I will not answer; they shall seek me early, but they shall not find me: For that they hated knowledge, and did not choose the fear of the Lord: They would none of my counsel: they despised all my reproof. Therefore shall they eat of the fruit of their own way, and be filled with their own devices. For the turning away of the simple shall slay them, and the prosperity of fools shall destroy them. (Proverbs 1:24–32)

- *Repentance*

Repentance also helps us to lighten up. It is by repentance that we receive the oil of God's Spirit. "Then Peter said unto them, Repent, and be baptized every one of you in the name of Jesus Christ for the remission of sins, and ye shall receive the gift of the Holy Ghost" (Acts 2:38). Whenever we genuinely repent, God in return sends us fresh drafts of His Spirit. Receiving more oil, our lamps burn brighter. Of course, repentance is the work of "trimming" sin from our hearts. Repentance is the elimination of the soot from the heart. Hence, *repentance helps us to lighten up.*

The five foolish virgins, in failing to repent, failed to obtain the Holy Spirit. They did not seek repentance in a time when it was available.

Follow peace with all men, and holiness, without which no man shall see the Lord: Looking diligently lest any man fail of the grace of God; lest any root of bitterness springing up trouble you, and thereby many be defiled; Lest there be any fornicator, or profane person, as Esau, who for one morsel of meat sold his birthright. For ye know how that afterward, when he would have inherited the blessing, he was rejected: for he found no place of repentance, though he sought it carefully with tears. (Hebrews 12:14–17)

- *Empty and Pour*

The emptying of self and the sharing of the spirit of God with others is crucial to our fires burning brighter. This is vividly illustrated in another "oil story." In the time of Elisha, there was a widow who was in debt. Having nothing but one pot of oil, Elisha told her:

Go, borrow thee vessels abroad of all thy neighbours, even empty vessels; borrow not a few. And when thou art come in, thou shalt shut the door upon thee and upon thy sons, and shalt pour out into all those vessels, and thou shalt set aside that which is full. So she went from him, and shut the door upon her and upon her sons, who brought the vessels to her; and she poured out. And it came to pass, when the vessels were full, that she said unto her son, Bring me yet a vessel. And he said unto her, There is not a vessel more. And the oil stayed. (2 Kings 4:3–6)

Only empty vessels can be used by the Lord. We must empty ourselves so that the spirit can dwell within us. Also, the vessels portray the work of evangelism. We should, like the widow, seek to share what we have with others who are seeking. The moment we cease to share what God has so graciously bestowed upon us, we are in danger of the oil ceasing to flow. *Emptying and pouring helps us to lighten up.*

In refusing to lighten up, or let their light shine, in refusing to share what they received from God, the five foolish virgins eliminated themselves from the preaching work of the loud cry. In a time of crisis, they sought to shine but were unable to do so. It is a work only the wise participated in. "They that be wise shall shine as the brightness of the firmament; and they that turn many to righteousness as the stars for ever and ever" (Daniel 12:3).

- *Forgiving Love*
Solomon told us that love is like a fire that cannot be quenched (see Song of Solomon 8:6–8). Love is often best demonstrated in our capacity to forgive those who have hurt us. Satan wants to snuff out our love through our own iniquity, or the iniquity of others toward us. "Because iniquity shall abound, the love of many shall wax cold. But he that shall endure unto the end, the same shall be saved" (Matthew 24:12, 13). The five wise virgins "endured" because their fire, or love, had not gone cold, despite the treatment they received at the hands of others.

The five foolish "wax cold." Their fire (love) went out. By hating, despising, evil surmising, and an unforgiving spirit, the five foolish virgins eliminated themselves from the very thing they needed in their time of trouble. As they went to buy oil, what they were really asking for was that their sins be forgiven.

Remember, it is by repentance that the oil is received. Repentance is the act of asking for forgiveness, but they were denied the oil. Why? Not only because probation had closed at that time, but also because they failed to forgive others.

How often we feel that we have been dealt with unjustly, that things have been said concerning us that were untrue, and that we have been set in a false light before others. When we are thus tried, we shall need to keep strict guard over our spirit and our words. We shall need to have the love of Christ, that we may not cherish an unforgiving spirit. Let us not think that unless those who have injured us confess their wrongs, we are justified in withholding from them our forgiveness. We should not accumulate our grievances, holding them to our hearts until the one we think guilty has humbled his heart by repentance and confession. ... However sorely they may have wounded us, we are not to cherish our grievances and sympathize with ourselves over our injuries, but as we hope to be pardoned for our offenses against God, so must we pardon those who have done evil to us. ...

When we are reviled, how strong is the temptation to revile in return, but in doing this we show ourselves as bad as the reviler. When tempted to revile, send up a silent prayer that God will give you His grace, and keep the tongue in silence. (*Youth's Instructor*, June 1, 1893)

Yes, love helps us to lighten up. The five foolish virgins wait until it's too late before they take Bible study seriously; before they decide to pray as if their lives depended on it; before they decide to confess all known sins and secret sins, making things right with those they have wronged; before they decide to empty themselves for the sake of others being filled; before they decide to forgive as they hoped to be forgiven. The foolish part of it all is that all this they could have done before it was too late, but they simply chose not to.

Group Discussion Questions

1. What impacted you most from this chapter?
2. Why is trimming the lamp vital?
3. Discuss the mistakes of the five foolish virgins.
4. Discuss the wisdom of the five wise virgins.

Chapter 7
Arise and Shine

Oone of Jesus' last prayers is recorded in the book of John where he pled with His Father. He beseeched, "The hour is come; glorify thy Son, that thy Son also may glorify thee: and now, O Father, glorify thou me with thine own self with the glory which I had with thee before the world was" (John 17:1, 3). He also prayed that this same glory, with which he was to be glorified, would be given to those who should follow Him afterward. "The glory which thou gavest me I have given them; that they may be one, even as we are one" (John 17:22). It was this glory that was to lighten the world.

Immediately after this prayer, Jesus went to the garden of Gethsemane, to *pray again*: "When Jesus had spoken these words, he went forth with his disciples over the brook Cedron, where was a garden, into the which he entered, and his disciples" (John 18:1). This time His prayer seemed to be in response to an answer *already given*. He then prayed, "O my Father, if it be possible, let this cup pass from me: nevertheless not as I will, but as thou wilt" (Matthew 26:39).

Christ prayed to be glorified; then He asked if there was any other way glorification could occur. The answer was no. There was only one way for Christ to be glorified, and in this glorification was the saving of untold numbers. In fact, God had answered the prayer of Jesus in the Scriptures hundreds of years before Christ's prayer was uttered. God spoke these words through the prophet Isaiah saying to His Son:

> Arise, shine; for thy light is come, and the glory of the Lord is risen upon thee. For, behold, the darkness shall cover the earth, and gross darkness the people: but the Lord shall arise upon thee, and his glory shall be seen upon thee. And the Gentiles shall come to thy light, and kings to the brightness of thy rising. (Isaiah 60:1–3)

> Behold my servant, whom I uphold; mine elect, in whom my soul delighteth; I have put my spirit upon him: he shall bring forth judgment to the Gentiles. I the Lord have called thee in righteousness, and will hold thine hand, and will keep thee, and give thee for a covenant of the people, for a light of the Gentiles;

To open the blind eyes, to bring out the prisoners from the prison, and them that sit in darkness out of the prison house. (Isaiah 42:1, 6, 7 emphasis added)

In order for Christ to be glorified, the candle, the light of the world, must be set on a candlestick—the light must be set on a hill—so that all could see it. So Christ said, "I, if I be lifted up from the earth, will draw all men unto me" John 12:32. Christ needed to "arise" in order to shine. There was no other way. "Upon the world's dark night the Sun of Righteousness must rise, 'with healing in His wings.' Malachi 4:2" (*The Desire of Ages*, 22). See his arms stretched out upon the cross. There His healing wings would provide for all who would humbly go before Him.

Indeed at the cross darkness covered the people. "Now from the sixth hour there was darkness over all the land unto the ninth hour" (Matthew 27:45). Then "suddenly the gloom lifted from the cross, and in clear, trumpet-like tones, that seemed to resound throughout creation, Jesus cried, 'It is finished.' 'Father, into Thy hands I commend My spirit.' *A light encircled the cross, and the face of the Saviour shone with a glory like the sun*. He then bowed His head upon His breast, and died" (*The Desire of Ages*, 756, emphasis added). "For God, who commanded the light to shine out of darkness, hath shined in our hearts, to give the light of the knowledge of the glory of God in the face of Jesus Christ" (2 Corinthians 4:5, 6).

In the act of the cross, Christ demonstrated that the only way for us to share in His glory, the glory that is to lighten the world, was to first "arise." That is, we too must be lifted up on the cross. We too must take up our cross and follow Him to the hill called Calvary. To do this, Christ had to humble himself. "Being found in fashion as a man, he humbled himself, and became obedient unto death, even the death of the cross. Wherefore God also hath highly exalted him, and given him a name which is above every name" (Philippians 2:8, 9).

A proud man or woman will fight being lifted up on a cross. He or she will fight the shame that comes with it. He will fight the vulnerability of being nailed to a cross, where the unsanctified in heart will take all the shots they can. Christ *rose above* the taunting, the spitting, the cursing, *He was above it all*! Despite the hatred shown to Him, He kept His arms open wide. Herein is the key to *victory over sin, over the world, over worldliness, and over our enemies*. It is to *rise above it all through the cross*. Christ was lifted up from the earth. If we too would shine, we too must be lifted up from this world and its lusts and wickedness. Rise above the lust, the anger. We must drop the attitude, and get some altitude. *Arise, and then you will shine.*

James wrote, "Humble yourselves in the sight of the Lord, and he shall lift you up" (James 4:10, emphasis added). That is, get rid of the pride that stops you from accepting the shame of humility, stop fighting the cross. "The two thieves wrestled in the hands of those who placed them on the cross; but Jesus made no resistance" (*The Desire of Ages*, 744). Jesus humbled Himself, but the pride of the two thieves caused them to fight being lifted up. Humble yourself, *so that*, the Lord can *lift you up*. There, lifted up on the cross, there the glory of the Lord shall be raise you up. This glory, the secret to victory over sin through Christ, is what will lighten the world, and be as a "light to the Gentiles" (Isaiah 49:6).

> The Gentiles shall come to thy light, and kings to the brightness of *thy rising*. ... Then thou shalt see, and flow together, and thine heart shall fear, and be enlarged; because the abundance of the sea shall be converted unto thee, the forces of the Gentiles shall come unto thee. (Isaiah 60:3, 5)

Of course Satan does not want the virgins to arise because in so doing they will reveal the light of Christ crucified as the key to victory over sin and over self. So his tactic is to try to get us to get down—"*Get Down*." In the world the term means the ability to do bad things well.

A person who knows how to fight, how to fight dirty, is said to know how to "get down." It's too bad that many Christians know how to "get down." They know how to hate, hold grudges, gossip, and backbite. The Pharisees knew how to "get down." Judas knew how to "get down." Satan and his forces at the cross tried to get Jesus to "get down": "If thou be the Son of God, come down from the cross" (Matthew 27:40). Jesus, however, refused to get down. The lesson is a powerful one. Christ is "able to keep you from falling" (Jude 24). In fact, *it is impossible to fall off the cross*. One must intentionally remove the Spirit that holds him or her up there to "get down." We need to sustain our altitude and not be always having an up-and-down experience.

> In the parable of the virgins, five were found wise and five foolish. Can it be possible that half of us will be found without the oil of grace in our lamps? Shall we come to the marriage feast too late? We have slept too long; shall we sleep on, and be lost at last? Are there those here who have been sinning and repenting, sinning and repenting, and will they continue to do so till Christ shall come? May God help us that we may be truly united to Christ, the living vine, and bear fruit to the glory of God! Many feel rich, and regard themselves as in need of nothing; but may

such confess their sins, and let the Spirit of God into their hearts. O, let us fear to go on in our evil, unrepenting state, lest we become like Judas, and finally betray our blessed Lord! (*The Review and Herald*, April 21, 1891)

Only those who learn how to rise, to be lifted up "from the earth" *now* through the cross, will be in that number that "rise" *from the earth* when Jesus comes again (see 1 Thessalonians 4:13–17). When the five wise virgins "go in" to the wedding feast, a symbol of the second coming, they had *risen to Christ* because they had practiced *rising with Christ*. The five foolish cannot go to the wedding because they did not know how to rise; only self had been trained to be lifted up.

This is the problem with the foolish virgins. They get down off the cross at the slightest provocation and the slightest temptation. *They do not rise on the cross and, therefore, do not shine.* They do not sustain the altitude of the cross. Instead of remaining lifted upon the cross, these *allow self to rise*. And whenever self rises, glory cannot.

The two thieves on the cross were both lifted up. One became wise. The other remained foolish. The wise humbled himself and stopped fighting to get off the cross. His request was simple: "Lord, remember me when you come into your kingdom" (Luke 23:42). Here he signaled that he was no longer fighting against the cross but had embraced it, gripped it. The foolish thief fought until the end. His appeal: "Save thyself and us" (Luke 23:39) had the appearance of a desire to be saved, but like the five foolish virgins' request for oil, it was based upon self rising, self preservation.

The two thieves may represent the two classes in our parable. All ten virgins in our parable "arose." "Then all those virgins arose and trimmed their lamps. And the foolish said unto the wise, Give us of your oil; for our lamps are gone out" (Matthew 25:7, 8). Five rose and the glory of the Lord was seen upon them. They shined.

The Gentiles will be converted unto them because God's people reflect a brighter light. Their message is pointing to Christ lifted up on the cross, the Light of the world. The message of the five wise virgins points to that Light as the only way to salvation, to the forgiveness of sins, and to the keeping from sin. As they shared this light, others took hold of it, and experienced "the glory of the Lord," thus lighting the whole world. The light was not only in their tongues but also in their hearts.

The foolish had lamps, but had no oil in their vessels with their lamps. Those represented by this class will die greater sinners than they were before they professed to believe the truth, because when they knew God, they worshipped Him not as God. Self, self, self, in all its perverted attributes, hardened the heart and closed the door against Jesus Christ, that He should not enter and abide with them. (*Manuscript Releases*, 37)

The five foolish also arose, but it was all "self." No glory shined upon them. May God help us at last to arise, so that we may shine with the glory of the Lord instead of reflecting the folly of sin, self and darkness.

Group Discussion Questions

1. What impacted you most about this chapter?

2. Discuss the significance of "rising" before one can shine.

3. Discuss the difference between rising and shining and self rising up. How do the two principles play themselves out on a daily basis?

4. How can we stay "lifted up" on the cross?

Chapter 8
Delay Reveals Character

In this chapter we will study an amazing parallel between an Old Testament story and the parable of the ten virgins. Moses had led the children of Israel out of Egyptian captivity. They were declared by God Himself to be His chosen nation.

> Now therefore, if ye will obey my voice indeed, and keep my covenant, then ye shall be a peculiar treasure unto me above all people: for all the earth is mine: and ye shall be unto me a kingdom of priests, and an holy nation. These are the words which thou shalt speak unto the children of Israel. (Exodus 19:5, 6)

Shortly after this, God called Moses up into the mount to receive instruction for the people.

> Moses rose up, and his minister Joshua: and Moses went up into the mount of God. And he said unto the elders, Tarry ye here for us, until we come again unto you: and, behold, Aaron and Hur are with you: if any man have any matters to do, let him come unto them. And Moses went up into the mount, and a cloud covered the mount. (Exodus 24:14, 15).

A cloud took Moses out of the sight of the people. Before Moses left, he had instructed the elders that there would be a tarrying time until he would "come again." Moses went up into the mount and into the cloud where he tarried longer than the people below had expected. Thus, the background was set for the events of Exodus, chapter 32.

> When the people saw that Moses delayed to come down out of the mount, the people gathered themselves together unto Aaron, and said unto him, Up, make us gods, which shall go before us; for as for this Moses, the man that brought us up out of the land of Egypt, we wot not what is become of him. (Exodus 32:1, 2)

The delay of the return of Moses led those who were unsanctified in heart to reveal their true characters. These foolish ones made a golden calf and began to worship it in the name of "the Lord" (Exodus 32:5).

> Aaron said unto them, Break off the golden earrings, which are in the ears of your wives, of your sons, and of your daughters, and bring them unto me. And all the people brake off the golden earrings which were in their ears, and brought them unto Aaron. And he received them at their hand, and fashioned it with a graving tool, after he had made it a molten calf: and they said, These be thy gods, O Israel, which brought thee up out of the land of Egypt. And when Aaron saw it, he built an altar before it; and Aaron made proclamation, and said, *To morrow is a feast to the Lord.* And they rose up early on the morrow, and offered burnt offerings, and brought peace offerings; and the people sat down to eat and to drink, and rose up to play. (Exodus 32:2–6, emphasis added)

The people who were entertaining themselves under the disguise of worship were caught off guard at Moses' *unexpected* return. Those not participating in this worship were looking and hoping, no doubt, for Moses to return. Upon his return those who were unprepared and who had made their decision against Moses, while declaring to worship the Lord, were separated from those who were on the Lord's side. "Then Moses stood in the gate of the camp, and said, Who is on the Lord's side? let him come unto me. And all the sons of Levi gathered themselves together unto him" (Exodus 32:26).

> Those who had not joined in the apostasy were to take their position at the right of Moses; those who were guilty but repentant, at the left. The command was obeyed. It was found that the tribe of Levi had taken no part in the idolatrous worship. From among other tribes there were great numbers who, although they had sinned, now signified their repentance. But a large company, mostly of the mixed multitude that instigated the making of the calf, stubbornly persisted in their rebellion. In the name of "the Lord God of Israel," Moses now commanded those upon his right hand, who had kept themselves clear of idolatry, to gird on their swords and slay all who persisted in rebellion. (*Patriarchs and Prophets*, 324)

After this separation, those who were guilty of apostasy, continued in their rebellion, and stood on the left hand of Moses were slain. On the right of Moses stood the Levites who, having kept themselves from the idolatrous worship of these unwise Israelites, were given the honor of doing service in God's temple. "God had honored the Levites to do service in the tabernacle, because they took no part in making and worshiping the golden calf, and because of their faithfulness in executing the order of God upon the idolaters. (*The Spirit of Prophecy*, vol. 1, 296)

This Old Testament account carries great significance or us today. It is indeed the parable of the ten virgins acted out. The ten virgins, the true church, had been led out of Babylonian captivity, a period lasting 1,260 years. Soon after Israel began its journey out of Egypt, they received God's law at Sinai, the Ten Commandments as the standard of righteousness. Likewise, soon after the church of God emerged from the persecution of the dark ages, they too received the law of God.

After October 22, 1844, God's people began to understand that Jesus had entered into the presence of God, ushered in by clouds, just as Moses had been taken into the presence of God, covered by a cloud. "I saw in the night visions, and, behold, one like the Son of man came with the clouds of heaven, and came to the Ancient of days, and they brought him near before him" (Daniel 7:13). The ten virgins were energized by this light that Christ had indeed entered the most holy place, so they went forth preaching that the Bridegroom would soon come.

Then there was a delay. Bitterly disappointed that they did not see Jesus face to face, they experienced a "tarrying time." During this "tarrying time," the character of the foolish virgins was exposed. The characters of the five foolish virgins became readily apparent during the "tarrying time" because they were not prepared for the delay. Here we see that delay reveals character.

When the ten virgins went forth to meet the bridegroom, their lamps were trimmed and burning. Apparently there was no difference between the five who were wise and the five who were foolish. To outward appearance all were prepared, robed in white, and carrying their lighted lamps. But only five of these virgins were wise. These anticipated delay, and filled their flagons with oil, ready for any emergency. Five of the number had not this foresight; they made no provision for disappointment or delay. (*The Review and Herald*, October 31, 1899)

Just as the foolish Israelites grew impatient for the return of Moses and turned to entertaining themselves under the disguise of worshipping

God, so many are doing now. "The foolish had lamps, but had no oil in their vessels with their lamps. Those represented by this class will die greater sinners than they were before they professed to believe the truth, because when they knew God, *they worshipped Him not as God*" (*Manuscript Releases*, vol. 21, 37, emphasis added).

The children of Israel decided to worship as the Egyptians did but in the name of "the Lord." Their music, their worship, their activities all pointed to Egypt, but they insisted that their worship was "of the Lord." In actuality, it was self entertainment. The foolish virgins did the same in the name of "the Lord." Instead of using the lamp of the cross and the three angels' messages to win souls, they turned to other methods of worship in order to gain influence. Since Christ, like Moses, has delayed His coming, many are content to entertain themselves. However, so they do not to seem irreligious, they claim that their worship is in the name of the Lord.

The foolish virgins of today are not looking for Jesus' imminent return. The wise virgins, who do not lash out at the foolish, only pray, plead, hope, and look for the coming of the Lord. When the Bridegroom does come, the foolish will be caught unprepared. Then the question "who is on the Lord's side" will not be asked, but rather answered by the Lord.

> When the Son of man shall come in his glory, and all the holy angels with him, then shall he sit upon the throne of his glory: And before him shall be gathered all nations: and he shall separate them one from another, as a shepherd divideth his sheep from the goats: And he shall set the sheep on his right hand, but the goats on the left. (Matthew 25:31–33)

The goats on the left, the five foolish virgins, and all the lost will be slaughtered, not by the wise, but by the "brightness" of the coming of the Lord. The very light that they should have embraced will destroy them. Just as the Levites who did not participate in the idolatry of those professing to know God were given the honors of service in the temple, so the five wise virgins will go into the wedding feast, and they will "serve him day and night in his temple" (Revelation 7:15) where "they shall be priests of God and of Christ, and shall reign with him a thousand years" (Revelation 20:6). Let us heed the lesson we can learn from the foolish errors of those who worshipped in the spirit of Egypt while claiming the name "of the Lord."

Group Discussion Questions

1. What impacted you most about this chapter?

2. How does delay reveal character?

3. What are the modern day idols Satan seeks to bring into the church under the name of "the Lord?"

4. What should the people of God be doing in this time of delay?

Chapter 9
Standing Before Jordan

First Corinthians 10:11 records these words: "Now all these things happened unto them for ensamples: and they are written for our admonition, upon whom the ends of the world are come."

By looking at the history of the church in the wilderness, we may understand where we are in the prophetic timeline at the close of earth's history. By understanding the successes and failures of ancient Israel, we may avoid repeating their failures while building on their successes. In this chapter, we will look at the history of the exodus to Canaan to find clues as to why we have not yet entered the heavenly Promised Land, as well as glean some very important lessons concerning the latter rain.

To start, let us trace the history, beginning with the exodus from Egypt. It began with the sacrifice of a lamb, through which the ancient church found deliverance, or a way out—exodus—from bondage (Exodus 12). Shortly afterward, the Old Testament church passed through the Red Sea (Exodus 14). After they began their journey into the wilderness, God said, "Ye have seen what I did unto the Egyptians, and how I bare you on eagles' wings, and brought you unto myself" (Exodus 19:4). After forty years in the wilderness, the children of Israel prepared to enter Canaan, the Promised Land, but before they could enter, they needed to cross the intimidating, rushing Jordan River (Joshua 3).

The parallel is stunning. The New Testament church had its beginning through the sacrifice of the Lamb of God. In John 14:6, Jesus declared Himself "the way" (Greek: *hodos*, as in Exodus). Next, just as the Old Testament church was baptized through the Red Sea, so the New Testament church, shortly after its freedom from the bondage of sin through the blood of the Lamb, was baptized by the symbolic waters of the early rain on the day of Pentecost (see Acts 2). "Moreover, brethren, I would not that ye should be ignorant, how that all our fathers were under the cloud, and all passed through the sea; and were all baptized unto Moses in the cloud and in the sea" (1 Corinthians 10:1, 2).

After the Old Testament church crossed the Red Sea, the people spent a long period in the wilderness, borne up on "eagles' wings." In the same manner, after the early church had experienced the early rain, they spent "1,260 years in the wilderness" (Revelation 12) borne up on "eagles' wings." "To the woman were given two wings of a great eagle, that she might fly into the wilderness, into her place, where she is nourished for a time, and times, and half a time, from the face of the serpent" (Revelation 12:4).

As Seventh-day Adventists, we understand that the wilderness period of 1,260 years ended in 1798. However, we have not yet entered Canaan. So where are we in the antitype? *We are standing just before the River Jordan*. Here, we have powerful lessons to learn concerning our location in the antitype.

First, just as the Red Sea was a symbol of baptism, finding its counterpart in the early rain baptism of Acts 2, so the Jordan must also be a type of baptism, finding its counterpart in the final outpouring of the Holy Spirit also known as the latter rain. So what is the hold up? Why do we seem to be hesitating before the mighty Jordan? We have been out of the wilderness phase since 1798, and as a church, we have grasped the understanding of our final mission to take the three angels' messages to the entire world to bring about the fall of Babylon through the loud cry. So why have we not yet crossed the Jordan to claim the Promised Land?

Consider the crossing of the Red Sea and the crossing of the Jordan as two contrasting experiences. At the Red Sea, Moses lifted up his rod, parting the waters so that the children of Israel could cross through it. Young in faith, *they had to see before they believed and acted.* Remember, just like the children of Israel waited for God to act, the disciples "tarried" in Jerusalem *until God moved* (see Acts 1, 2).

The crossing of the Jordan, however, would be an opposite experience. God's people needed to demonstrate their faith by stepping into the raging waters *before the waters would part.* They needed to believe and act *before* they could see. Had the children of Israel stood by, waiting for the river to part or waiting for a miraculous event, they would have never crossed. Could it be that while we are waiting for some signal, some supernatural manifestation of God's power to indicate the final outpouring of the Holy Spirit to move us to act and believe, that God is actually waiting on us to exercise faith, to believe, and to act *before* we see the supernatural moving of God?

Many Seventh-day Adventists have been told and believe that we are waiting for the time of trouble to come upon us. But could it be the other way around? Could the time of trouble be waiting for us? Remember what was on the other side of the Jordan? A time of trouble! In fact, you will recall, Moses sent twelve men, including Joshua and Caleb, to spy on the Promised Land (see Numbers 13, 14). When the spies returned, ten of them delivered troublesome news:

They brought up an evil report of the land which they had searched unto the children of Israel, saying, The land, through which we have gone to search it, is a land that eateth up the inhabitants thereof; and all the people that we saw in it are men of a great stature. And there we saw the giants, the sons of Anak, which come of the giants: and we were in our own sight as grasshoppers, and so we were in their sight. (Numbers 13:32, 33)

This fear of the trouble that lay on the other side of the River Jordan kept the people from desiring to cross over into the Promised Land.

All the congregation lifted up their voice, and cried; and the people wept that night. And all the children of Israel murmured against Moses and against Aaron: and the whole congregation said unto them, Would God that we had died in the land of Egypt! or would God we had died in this wilderness! And wherefore hath the Lord brought us unto this land, to fall by the sword, that our wives and our children should be a prey? were it not better for us to return into Egypt? And they said one to another, Let us make a captain, and let us return into Egypt. (Numbers 14:1–4)

In like manner, could it be that what keeps the people of God from the baptism of the latter rain of the Holy Spirit is an unpreparedness and fearfulness of moving forward into the time of trouble? Could it be that like the unfaithful spies, we would rather live life in the wilderness, or worse, in Egypt? Many today would rather that their children get to experience the wilderness, or worse Egypt, rather than cross over into a time of trouble. We like the comforts, the luxuries, and the amenities of life. Who wants trouble?

The ten spies saw trouble. Joshua and Caleb, however, saw the land of promise.

Joshua the son of Nun, and Caleb the son of Jephunneh, which were of them that searched the land, rent their clothes: And they spake unto all the company of the children of Israel, saying, The land, which we passed through to search it, is an exceeding good land. If the Lord delight in us, then he will bring us into this land, and give it us; a land which floweth with milk and honey. Only rebel not ye against the Lord, neither fear ye the people of the land; for they are bread for us: their defence is departed from them, and the Lord is with us: fear them not. (Numbers 14:7–9)

Joshua and Caleb desired to advance into what others saw clearly as a time of trouble. What is the attitude of our church today? Is it one of desiring to advance toward the Promised Land, never minding the time of trouble we will face along the way? Or is it a desire like that of the ten spies to wait it out, to continue life as normal in the wilderness, or worse, return to the land of Egypt? The five foolish virgins possessed the same attitude as the ten unfaithful spies. They were unprepared to advance in the face of crisis. They would rather have rested than act. They were more comfortable being lukewarm instead of burning brightly.

The next lesson to learn is vital. The Jordan River did not dry up for the twelve spies. It dried up when the people as a whole decided to cross over. For too long, the church has been sending "spies," key individuals, into enemy territory to snatch souls from the kingdom of darkness. Our big name preachers, teachers, and evangelists, time and time again, go out to the battlefield, in the depths of enemy territory. They return with fruit taken from the grip of Satan's kingdom. They share thrilling reports of their ventures—50 baptisms here, 1,000 baptisms there. Praise God! But the Jordan will not dry up; the latter rain will not come until we decide as a united front to cross the Jordan into the time of trouble. The Promise Land is right before us, and we need to step into the Jordan by faith.

When we cease our dependence on a "spy" here and there, and as a people decide to cross the Jordan, then God will answer our faith by sending the rain.

> The great outpouring of the Spirit of God, which lightens the whole earth with His glory, will not come until we have an enlightened people, that know by experience what it means to be laborers together with God. When we have entire, whole-hearted consecration to the service of Christ, God will recognize the fact by an outpouring of His Spirit without measure; but this will not be while the largest portion of the church are not laborers together with God. (*The Review and Herald*, July 21, 1896, emphasis added)

We should not fail to see the connection between the ark of the covenant and the "baptism" through the Jordan. The priests carried the ark, upon which rested the mercy seat flanked by the "two anointed ones." These covering cherubs, according to Zechariah (see chapter 5), emptied the oil into the burning lamps. In like manner, God's spiritual priesthood will go forth, bearing the message of light specifically pointing to the law of God, the intercession of Christ in the most holy place. They will go forth filled with the oil flowing from the two anointed ones who minister the "oil of grace" that enables their lamps to burn to prepare a people for the coming of the Bridegroom. When we as a people understand the importance of the ark, its contents, and its message, as well as being prepared to unite simultaneously to take that message into enemy territory, then God will bless us. But we must step into the water. The Spirit is waiting for us to advance with purpose.

The crossing of the Jordan occurred at the time of the harvest—"for Jordan overfloweth all his banks all the time of harvest" (Joshua 3:15). It is not coincidence that the outpouring of the latter rain will, indeed, be at the time of great harvest. "The work will be similar to that of the Day of Pentecost. As the "'former rain'" was given, in the outpouring of the Holy Spirit at the opening of the gospel, to cause the upspringing of the precious seed, so the "'latter rain'" will be given at its close, for the ripening of the harvest" (*The Great Controversy*, 611).

Because of their unbelief, the people were told that their generation would die in the wilderness. Could it be our unbelief, our inability to grasp by faith the nearness of the Promised Land before us, that has led to generation after generation dying without seeing the outpouring of God's Spirit?

It was much later after that generation had died in the wilderness that Joshua prepared the people to enter into Canaan, to enter into battle, and they had a plan. Until the people of God unite upon a plan, we are simply acting as independent atoms.

> Those who belong to Christ's army must work with concerted action. They cannot be faithful soldiers unless they obey orders. United action is essential. An army in which every part acts without reference to the other parts, has no real strength. In order to add new territory to Christ's kingdom, His soldiers must act in concert. ... He calls for a united army, which moves steadily forward, not for a company composed of independent atoms. The strength of His army is to be used for one great purpose. Its efforts are to be concentrated upon one great point—the magnifying of the laws of His kingdom before the world, before angels, and before men. (*Manuscript Releases*, vol. 20, 28)

> If each member of the church felt an interest to bless and benefit the church, he would have a keen anxiety to see it prosper. It is simple mismanagement that demoralizes our churches. It is because the members of the church do not act their part with fidelity, that the cause of truth is not further advanced. Development

and discipline are essential if we would see growth and prosperity in every church. There must be concerted action, and the members of the church must move together like a band of well-trained soldiers. The mind requires constant discipline in order to be trained to do acceptable work for Jesus. The mental faculties must be constantly expanded by exercise, that their highest usefulness may be developed. If church members are educated to be silent and useless members, instead of benefiting the church, they will be a hindrance to its advancement and growth. If they are educated to lean upon the minister, they will become only inefficient and demoralized members, and the church will be powerless, instead of active and efficient. (*The Review and Herald*, October 22, 1889)

After Israel crossed the Jordan, they knew they were entering into a time of trouble. But God was with them. They brought down Jericho, not by might, nor by power, but by God's Spirit. Jericho was brought down by a loud shout. So the loud cry (the "midnight cry" in the parable of the ten virgins) that brought about the fall of Babylon can only occur after we have crossed the spiritual Jordan, having been baptized with the Holy Spirit. Then we shall go forth in the power of God's Spirit to give the loud cry.

One final note should be mentioned. When Joshua himself sent two spies into Jericho, a harlot named Rahab met them with peace and assisted them. Yet, she stayed in Jericho until the entire army of Israel came forth. In like manner, God has many Rahabs who are currently living in Babylon. They know the truth and believe it, just as did Rahab. However, it will not be until the Rahabs, God's people who are currently part of the harlot Babylon, see the entire army of God crossing the Jordan that they will respond by "coming out" and joining the people of God.

I heard those clothed with the armor speak forth the truth with great power. It had effect. Many had been bound; some wives by their husbands, and some children by their parents. The honest who had been prevented from hearing the truth now eagerly laid hold upon it. All fear of their relatives was gone, and the truth alone was exalted to them. They had been hungering and thirsting for truth; it was dearer and more precious than life. I asked what had made this great change. An angel answered, "It is the latter rain, the refreshing from the presence of the Lord, the loud cry of the third angel." (*Early Writings*, 271)

The Rahabs today are waiting for the "midnight cry." Have we not kept them waiting long enough?

Group Discussion Questions

1. What parallel impacted you the most from this chapter?

2. What are some of the modern-day wilderness luxuries that cause the church to fear crossing the Jordan?

3. What do you think needs to happen for the church members to realize their individual responsibility for revival and the advancement of the church locally and globally?

4. What needs to happen for the church to understand the need for united movement?

Chapter 10
The Fourth Decree and the Fourth Angel's Message

I n this chapter we will study a second type, or parallel, tracing the history from 1 Chronicles to the book of Esther. The book of 1 Chronicles covers the history of Adam to the fall of Saul to the transition of the kingdom into David's hands, resulting in subsequent Israelite victories. David then prepared to build the temple; then his death is recorded.

A dim outline of the great controversy from Adam onward can be discerned here. Saul, who was once an "anointed" child of God (1 Samuel 15:1), eventually turned against God. He was a type of Satan, who was once an "anointed cherub," and he also turned against God (Ezekiel 28:14). Saul grew jealous of David and warred against him, Saul was eventually replaced by David as king of Israel. So too Satan grew jealous of Christ and warred against Him when He came to this earth, but Christ defeated Satan at the cross, becoming the rightful king of this earth.

As Saul was a type of Satan, so David was a type of Christ. David began to prepare the temple for his people, so Christ taught that He would go to prepare a place for His people (see John 14:1–3). David prepared for the temple but died before it was built; Christ died in order to go to prepare a place for us (see John 14:1–7).

Second Chronicles, chapters 1–9, cover the story of Solomon, son of David, who built the temple. Chapters 10–35 cover the division and apostasies that were pervasive throughout Israel. In the book's closing (chapter 36), Babylon had taken Israel captive, and the temple was cast down.

Again, a dim outline of the great controversy continues throughout this book. As Solomon, the son of David, began the work of building the temple, so Jesus Christ, *the Son of David* (Mark 12:35), ascended to heaven to begin the work of building the church. Soon after Solomon commenced upon the work of building the temple, divisions and apostasies plagued Israel. After Christ ascended to heaven to begin the work of building the church, divisions and apostasies began to enter the church. Paul called this apostasy, the "falling away" which in turn gave rise to the antichrist power prophesied by Paul as the "man of sin" (2 Thessalonians 2:3). Then just as Israel was taken captive by Babylon and its temple was cast down, so Mystery Babylon, or the "little horn" in the book of Daniel, "cast down" the "place" of God's temple in heaven and also held the church in captivity for 1,260 years (see Daniel 7:25; 8:11, 12).

The next two books, Ezra and Nehemiah, cover the four decrees or proclamations given to the Jews to rebuild their temple and city, something the Jews believed vital in preparing for the first coming of Christ. Amazingly, these four decrees correspond to the three angels' messages or proclamations found in Revelation 14:6—14 in connection with a fourth angel's proclamation found in Revelation 18:1–4. The prophetic chronology looks like this:

1. Adam submits to Satan (Saul)
2. Kingdom transitions from Satan (Saul) to David (Jesus)
3. David (Jesus) prepares to build a temple
4. Son of David (Jesus) builds the church: early church
5. Apostasies and divisions in Israel: the church
6. Babylon takes Jews captive, destroys the temple: Dark Ages
7. Four decrees given to assist Jews in rebuilding the temple: four angels' messages

The prophecy which pointed to the rebuilding of the temple and city is found in the ninth chapter of Daniel.

> Know therefore and understand, that from the going forth of the commandment to restore and to build Jerusalem unto the Messiah the Prince shall be seven weeks, and threescore and two weeks: the street shall be built again, and the wall, even in troublous times. (Daniel 9:25)

Four things were to be accomplished in the rebuilding of Jerusalem. These were the rebuilding of the temple, the rebuilding of the city, the rebuilding of the street, and the rebuilding of the wall, "even in troublous times."

Babylon was overthrown by Cyrus, king of the Persian Empire. After the defeat of Babylon, Cyrus issued a decree, or "proclamation," in 538 B.C., setting the Jews free to begin the work of rebuilding their temple. Though this decree is not the starting point of the prophecy of Daniel 9, it is a very significant decree, nonetheless.

> Now in the first year of Cyrus king of Persia, that the word of the Lord by the mouth of Jeremiah might be fulfilled, the Lord stirred up the spirit of Cyrus king of Persia, that he made a *proclamation* throughout all his kingdom, and put it also in writing, saying, Thus saith Cyrus king of Persia, The Lord God of heaven hath given me all the kingdoms of the earth; and he hath charged

me to build him an house at Jerusalem, which is in Judah. Who is there among you of all his people? his God be with him, and let him go up to Jerusalem, which is in Judah, and build the house of the Lord God of Israel, (he is the God,) which is in Jerusalem. (Ezra 1:1–3, emphasis added)

As a result of this first decree, we are informed that 50,000 Jews heeded the call. "The whole congregation together was forty and two thousand three hundred and threescore, beside their servants and their maids, of whom there were seven thousand three hundred thirty and seven: and there were among them two hundred singing men and singing women" (Ezra 2:64, 65).

Under the favor shown them by Cyrus, nearly fifty thousand of the children of the captivity had taken advantage of the decree permitting their return. (*Prophets and Kings*, 598)

This decree was specifically toward the work of rebuilding the temple. However, there was opposition to the work by the enemies of God's people (see Ezra 4), which led to the hindering of the first proclamation. Subsequently, a second decree was issued by King Darius of the Medes in 519 B.C. This decree was specifically against the enemies of the people of God. The second decree declared the fall, or pulling down, of the house of anyone opposing the first or second decree, or proclamation.

Now therefore, Tatnai, governor beyond the river, Shetharboznai, and your companions the Apharsachites, which are beyond the river, be ye far from thence: Let the work of this house of God alone; let the governor of the Jews and the elders of the Jews build this house of God in his place. ... Also I have made a decree, that whosoever shall alter this word, let timber be pulled down from his house, and being set up, let him be hanged thereon; and let his house be made a dunghill for this. And the God that hath caused his name to dwell there destroy all kings and people, that shall put to their hand to alter and to destroy this house of God which is at Jerusalem. I Darius have made a decree; let it be done with speed. (Ezra 6:6, 7, 11, 12)

God had even more favor in store for His chosen people. The first two decrees were concerning the temple and its building. A third decree was issued by Artaxerxes in 457 B.C. This decree went beyond the building of a temple and gave the Jews autonomy as a nation. This decree stated:

Thou, Ezra, after the wisdom of thy God, that is in thine hand, set magistrates and judges, which may judge all the people that are beyond the river, all such as know the laws of thy God; and teach ye them that know them not. And whosoever will not do the law of thy God, and the law of the king, let judgment be executed speedily upon him, whether it be unto death, or to banishment, or to confiscation of goods, or to imprisonment. (Ezra 7:25, 26)

Notice how this third decree, or proclamation, focused on the law of God and punishment for those who would not keep it. Under this decree, the Jews again became a separate and distinct society. This is the decree that we, as Seventh-day Adventists, focus on as the beginning of the 2,300 year prophecy found in Daniel 8 (457 B.C. to A.D. 1844).

Finally, there would be need for a fourth decree issued in 444 B.C. Under the third decree, discouragement had gripped the people of God, and the work lagged. Thirteen years after Artaxerxes' decree, we find this account by Nehemiah:

It came to pass in the month Chisleu, in the twentieth year, as I was in Shushan the palace, That Hanani, one of my brethren, came, he and certain men of Judah; and I asked them concerning the Jews that had escaped, which were left of the captivity, and concerning Jerusalem. And they said unto me, The remnant that are left of the captivity there in the province are in great affliction and reproach: the wall of Jerusalem also is broken down, and the gates thereof are burned with fire. (Nehemiah 1:1–3)

By messengers from Judea the Hebrew patriot learned that days of trial had come to Jerusalem, the chosen city. The returned exiles were suffering affliction and reproach. The temple and portions of the city had been rebuilt; but the work of restoration was hindered, the temple services were disturbed, and the people kept in constant alarm by the fact that the walls of the city were still largely in ruins. (*Prophets and Kings*, 628)

It was under these circumstances that a fourth and final decree was issued, again by King Artaxerxes. Notice that the fourth decree was really only an expansion of the third decree. Nehemiah's request was, "And I said unto the king, If it please the king, and if thy servant have found favour in thy sight, that thou wouldest send me unto Judah, unto the city of my fathers' sepulchres, that I may build it" (Nehemiah 2:5). The request was granted. Nehemiah completed the work of building and securing the wall in fifty-two days. "So the wall was finished in the twenty and fifth day of the month Elul, in fifty and two days." (Nehemiah 6:15) A work that lagged for 13 years was completed under Nehemiah in just fifty-two days.

Nehemiah's battle cry to the people was significant. "Then said I unto them, Ye see the distress that we are in, how Jerusalem lieth waste, and the gates thereof are burned with fire: come, and let us build up the wall of Jerusalem, that we be no more a reproach" (Nehemiah 2:17). *As long as the work lay incomplete, they were a reproach unto God.*

Just as there were four decrees or proclamations from the fall of Babylon, so there are four decrees or proclamations from the deadly wound received by spiritual Babylon in 1798. The four proclamations are the first, second, third, and fourth angels' messages. The parallels are beyond coincidence. Spiritual Babylon (see Revelation 17:5), the papal church, received a deadly wound in 1798; the once dominating and persecuting power of the Dark Ages was now toothless. The people of God in a special sense began to focus upon the prophecies of Daniel after the striking fulfillment in 1798. This study led to the prophecy of the 2,300 days which, in turn, led to the preaching of the first angel's message, a message that focused on the *sanctuary*, or temple, being cleansed or restored.

Ellen White wrote, "At the *proclamation* of the first angel's message, the people of God were in Babylon; and many true Christians are still to be found in her communion" (*The Spirit of Prophecy*, vol. 4, 239, emphasis added). What is even more interesting is that about fifty thousand Jews returned to Jerusalem under the first decree of Cyrus. When the first and second angels' messages were preached, we are told that "in the summer of 1844 about *fifty thousand* withdrew from the churches" (*The Great Controversy*, 375, emphasis added).

Just as the second decree or proclamation (by Darius) was given because of the opposition to the first decree, so the second angel's message was a warning of the impending fall of any church that dared to oppose the work of God in bringing attention to the sanctuary. Again, Ellen White wrote:

> As the churches refused to receive the first angel's message, they rejected the light from heaven and fell from the favor of God. They trusted to their own strength, and by opposing the first message placed themselves where they could not see the light of the second angel's message. But the beloved of God, who were oppressed, accepted the message, "Babylon is fallen," and left the churches. (*Early Writings*, 237)

It was under the third decree, however, that the Jews gained autonomy. An emphasis was placed upon the law of God, and a judgment was imposed against those who disobeyed it.

> Thou, Ezra, after the wisdom of thy God, that is in thine hand, set magistrates and judges, which may judge all the people that are beyond the river, all such as know the laws of thy God; and teach ye them that know them not. And whosoever will not do the law of thy God, and the law of the king, let judgment be executed speedily upon him, whether it be unto death, or to banishment, or to confiscation of goods, or to imprisonment. (Ezra 7:25, 26)

In like manner, the third angel's message, which began to be preached in about 1846, was given to identify the people of God. Under this third proclamation, the Seventh-day Adventist church was formally identified as its own autonomous entity. The third decree given by Artaxerxes was a combination and amplification of the first two decrees. So "the power of the proclamation of the first and second angels' messages is to be concentrated in the third" (*The Voice in Speech and Song*, 329). It also contains a warning for those who disregard the law.

> The third angel followed them, saying with a loud voice, If any man worship the beast and his image, and receive his mark in his forehead, or in his hand, the same shall drink of the wine of the wrath of God, which is poured out without mixture into the cup of his indignation; and he shall be tormented with fire and brimstone in the presence of the holy angels, and in the presence of the Lamb: and the smoke of their torment ascendeth up for ever and ever: and they have no rest day nor night, who worship the beast and his image, and whosoever receiveth the mark of his name. Here is the patience of the saints: here are they that keep the commandments of God, and the faith of Jesus. (Revelation 14:9–12)

If the parallels are correct, then as a people, we are awaiting one final decree, one final proclamation: the fourth angel's message, the message that is to complete the work of the people of God. Just as the fourth decree was a part of the third decree, so the fourth angel's message is really a part of the third. Speaking of the angel of Revelation 18:1–3, Ellen White wrote:

> The angel who *unites in the proclamation of the third angel's message* is to lighten the whole earth with his glory. A work of

worldwide extent and unwonted power is here foretold. The Advent movement of 1840–1844 was a glorious manifestation of the power of God; the first angel's message was carried to every missionary station in the world, and in some countries there was the greatest religious interest which has been witnessed in any land since the Reformation of the sixteenth century; but these are to be far exceeded by the mighty movement under the last *warning of the third angel.*

The work will be similar to that of the day of Pentecost. As the "former rain" was given, in the outpouring of the Holy Spirit at the opening of the gospel to cause the upspringing of the precious seed, so the "latter rain" will be given at its close, *for the ripening of the harvest.* (*The Great Controversy*, 610, 611, emphasis added)

The Work
The work to be accomplished under the fourth decree through Nehemiah is important to understand. The work of Nehemiah included rebuilding the "street" and the "wall." It was a work that would be accomplished "even in trouble times" (see Daniel 9:25). What is the antitype? What is the work that we, as God's last-day Nehemiah's, are to accomplish?

The Street
First, the street was to be rebuilt. "The street shall be built again, and the wall, even in troublous times" (Daniel 9:25). Notice that street is singular, indicating something very specific. What is the purpose of a street? It is to show *the way.*

There is no excuse for those who have the light of present truth, and yet fail to impart this light to others. God calls for workers. We have a great work to do in cooperating with Him as His helping hand and helping voice. Satan is casting his hellish shadow across the pathway of every soul, seeking to eclipse the testing truth for these last days. We are to sound the message of warning to a guilty race. We are to present to men the binding claims of God's law, so that when Christ comes they will not be found in disloyalty, on the side of the Apostate. *We must now prepare the way of the Lord. We must make plain in the desert a highway for our God.* (*The Upward Look*, 76, emphasis added)

The street that must be rebuilt is the street of salvation upon which the members of the church go up and down, proclaiming the message of the soon-coming Savior. We must show people the way to salvation, the way to the sanctuary, and the way to the city of God. If they are to leave Babylon, they must know what street to take in order to escape.

We must remove every hindrance that would keep us from traversing the street in search for every soul that will hear. The street has been damaged, even though few are traveling it. When the street has been fully repaired, the church will be seen actively traveling the highways and byways looking for souls that are lost, directing them toward spiritual Jerusalem.

An highway shall be there, and a way, and it shall be called The way of holiness; the unclean shall not pass over it; but it shall be for those: the wayfaring men, though fools, shall not err therein. (Isaiah 35:8)

As of now, the street has been damaged by the excuses of being unable to rightly articulate the faith, by our worldly desires and pursuits of other things, and by the fear of seeming out of place by warning that the Messiah is coming soon.

Go through, go through the gates; prepare ye the way of the people; cast up, cast up the highway; gather out the stones; lift up a standard for the people. Behold, the Lord hath proclaimed unto the end of the world, Say ye to the daughter of Zion, Behold, thy salvation cometh; behold, his reward is with him, and his work before him. (Isaiah 62:10, 11)

He knows whether we are clearing the King's highway from all rubbish and hindrance, so that He can beckon our souls onward and upward, or whether we are filling the path with rubbish and blocking up our own way, and placing stumbling blocks in the way of sinners to hinder the salvation of precious souls for whom Christ died. (*Mind, Character, and Personality*, vol. 2, 434)

This is the work of the five wise virgins. It is to show the way, which can be done only as they have light in a dark place—no lamps, no seeing which way to go. There is more to the reparation of the street. It is by this street that we are told the Lord will come. "God wants his church to take up the stones, to remove the rubbish, to clear the highway *for the coming of the Lord*. He wants them to prepare to meet their God" (*The General Conference Bulletin*, April 14, 1901, emphasis added).

Isaiah, the prophet, wrote, "The voice of him that crieth in the wilderness, Prepare ye the way of the Lord, make straight in the desert a highway for our God" (Isaiah 40:3). According to the book of Malachi, the Lord is coming some place specific. "Behold, I will send my messenger, and he shall prepare the way before me: and the Lord, whom ye seek, shall suddenly *come to his temple*" (Malachi 3:1, emphasis added). If we are temples according to the writings of Paul (see 1 Corinthians 3:16, 17, 6:19), then the highway leading to that temple is the heart.

This way, or street, must be cleared because it is the only avenue through which Christ, by the outpouring of the Holy Spirit, will be able to come to us to fill us. "Then shall we know, if we follow on to know the Lord: his going forth is prepared as the morning; *and he shall come unto us as the rain*, as the latter and former rain unto the earth" (Hosea 6:3, emphasis added). So this message, given by the five wise virgins, "the Bridegroom cometh" is also a message of the coming latter rain; a message that the foolish do not participate in.

> Clear the King's highway; take out the stumbling-blocks; remove the rubbish; clear away the stones, *that the Spirit of God may go through our midst,* and that we may see the salvation of God *as a lamp that burneth.* That is what we need. We can not afford to cover up one sin. We want the richest blessing here; for trial is coming right upon us. Only a little while, only a short time, and every one will be severely tried. We want a daily *renewal* of the grace of God *in our hearts*, that we may climb the ladder of perfection step by step, rising higher and higher in the way that leads to heaven, to holiness, and to God. (*The Review and Herald*, May 18, 1905, emphasis added)

> Let us, so far as possible, clear the King's highway of all the rubbish wherewith we have blocked it. (*The Review and Herald*, December 9, 1890)

Catch that point? In order for the street to be prepared, the avenue by which the Holy Spirit will move amongst the people of God, the rubbish must be cleared. *"We can not afford to cover up one sin."* A united work must be done to clear away the things that have blocked the Spirit from coming to us. This is the work of united confession, and the work of forgiving and letting go of grudges. It is the work of righteousness by faith. It is the work that is to be accomplished under the message of the fourth angel; or the fourth decree.

The Wall

The last phase of the work of Nehemiah was to complete the wall. The purpose of the wall was to be a defense for the city. When a city had no walls, it had no protection from outside attacks. As long as Jerusalem was without walls, 'its inhabitants lived in great fear. The walls were to defend the city in times of trouble and, in fact, was built in "troublous times" (see Daniel 9:25).

So what might these walls mean to us today under the fourth proclamation? The prophet Zechariah gives us this insight. "For I, saith the Lord, will be unto her a wall of fire round about, and will be the glory in the midst of her" (Zechariah 2:5). In other words, when the street has been cleared of all the rubbish, the Spirit of God will come in and act as a wall of fire, protecting the church from her enemies.

Nehemiah spent fifty-two days rebuilding the wall. Nehemiah also serves as a type of Christ. Just as Nehemiah was tempted to "come down" from his important work four times (see Nehemiah 6:1–4), so Christ was tempted four times upon the cross to come down from his work (by the priests, the Roman soldiers, the thief on the cross, and those that walked by). Just as Nehemiah responded, "I cannot come down, for I am doing a great work," so Christ refused to come down, for He too was doing a great work. Just as Nehemiah completed the wall in fifty-two days, so fifty-two days after Christ was on the cross, doing His "great work," He completed building a wall around His church, a wall of fire in the outpouring of the early rain (see Acts 2). Ellen White described the gift of the Holy Spirit this way:

> The gift of His Holy Spirit, rich, full, and abundant, is to be to His church as an encompassing wall of fire, which the powers of hell shall not prevail against. (*Testimonies to Ministers and Gospel Workers*, 18)

What does this tell us? That just as ancient Israel needed a wall of protection from her enemies, so Christ is waiting to pour out His Spirit to serve as a wall of protection around spiritual Israel. When the temple, the city, the street, and the wall are complete, then He allows the four winds of Revelation 7 to be loosed. Then God's people and city will be prepared for and protected against the onslaught of the enemy.

Amazingly, the history of 1 Chronicles through the book of Nehemiah covers the history of the great controversy down to the three angel's messages and the loud cry. But the book that follows Nehemiah, the book of Esther, reveals yet another parallel in this story.

Esther is about a man named Haman, who hated Mordecai because Mordecai was the only man who refused to bow down before him. Since

Haman could not get victory over Mordecai, he decided to attack the people of Mordecai (God's people), to wipe them out utterly by passing a death decree in language familiar to that found in describing the mark of the beast found in Revelation 13:15–17. "The letters were sent by posts into all the king's provinces, to destroy, to kill, and to cause to perish, all Jews, both young and old, little children and women, in one day" (Esther 3:13). But the virtuous woman Esther was brought upon the scene "for such a time as this" (Esther 4:14). Through her influence, Haman was defeated and also forced to reverence Mordecai.

In like manner, this entire world bowed to Satan's authority save one man, Jesus Christ, who refused to acknowledge his authority. Infuriated, Satan decided to go after the remnant (see Revelation 12) of God's people. Just as it happened in Esther's time, a death decree will be issued to wipe out the people of God in one decisive blow, but like Esther, a type of the virtuous bride of Christ, the church of God will be instrumental in proving Satan a liar and bring about his ultimate demise. Satan will be forced to acknowledge the supremacy of Christ. As God interceded for His people then, He is interceding for them now and will do so in the turbulent times ahead of that time of persecution and protection.

John the Revelator wrote:

> I saw four angels standing on the four corners of the earth, holding the four winds of the earth, that the wind should not blow on the earth, nor on the sea, nor on any tree. And I saw another angel ascending from the east, having the seal of the living God: and he cried with a loud voice to the four angels, to whom it was given to hurt the earth and the sea, saying, Hurt not the earth, neither the sea, nor the trees, till we have sealed the servants of our God in their foreheads. (Revelation 7:1–3)

God sees that we still have not completed the work; therefore, we are still unprepared for the final events, still unprepared to stand against Satan's decree to wipe out God's people. God is waiting for us to clear the street and repair the wall so that we may be kept "in troublous times."

What is most important to note, however, is the time it took Nehemiah to finish the work. *A work that had lagged on for thirteen years was completed in a matter of fifty-two days.* As a church we have been under the third angel's message since 1844. The work appears to be lagging. Every year that we celebrate another year of our existence, we become more of a "reproach" to God. What we need now is the spirit of Nehemiah. Those who will see the work lagging, will weep, and then do something about it.

The work of restoration and reform carried on by the returned exiles, under the leadership of Zerubbabel, Ezra, and Nehemiah, presents a picture of a work of spiritual restoration that is to be wrought in the closing days of this earth's history. ...

God's remnant people, standing before the world as reformers, are to show that the law of God is the foundation of all enduring reform and that the Sabbath of the fourth commandment is to stand as a memorial of creation, a constant reminder of the power of God. In clear, distinct lines they are to present the necessity of obedience to all the precepts of the Decalogue. Constrained by the love of Christ, they are to co-operate with Him in building *up the waste places. They are to be repairers of the breach, restorers of paths to dwell in.* (*Prophets and Kings*, 677, 678, emphasis added)

There is need of Nehemiahs in the church today,—not men who can pray and preach only, *but men whose prayers and sermons are braced with firm and eager purpose.* (*The Signs of the Times*, December 6, 1883, emphasis added)

Nehemiah had often poured out his soul in behalf of his people. But now as he prayed a holy purpose formed in his mind. He resolved that if he could obtain the consent of the king, and the necessary aid in procuring implements and material, *he would himself* undertake the task of rebuilding the walls of Jerusalem and restoring Israel's national strength. (*Prophets and Kings*, 629, 630, emphasis added}

Will you be a Nehemiah in your church to call the people to action?

Group Discussion Questions

1. Discuss the top three points that appealed to you in this chapter.
2. How can you become a Nehemiah?
3. What needs to occur in order for the "street" and "wall" to be completed?
4. What happens when the "street" and "wall" are completed?

Chapter 11
The Third Opening and the Coming Revival

As Seventh-day Adventists, we have long looked forward to the time of a promised revival to take place in our church. Verses such as Revelation 18:1–3; Joel 2:28; and James 5:7 have held a special place in the hearts of God's people. For more than 100 years we have waited and waited for the coming revival, yet it still tarries. Why?

In order to understand the coming revival, we must first understand its purpose. When Adam and Eve were created, they were able to dwell in the presence of God without shame or fear. "The holy pair were not only children under the fatherly care of God but students receiving instruction from the all-wise Creator. They were visited by angels, and were granted communion with their Maker, with no obscuring veil between" (*Patriarchs and Prophets*, 50).

When sin entered, a veil was placed between man and God. Isaiah recorded the following words: "but your iniquities have separated between you and your God, and your sins have hid his face from you, that he will not hear" (Isaiah 59:2).

Adam and Eve could no longer dwell in the presence of God. When He came to the garden looking for them, they "hid themselves from the presence of the Lord God" (Genesis 3:8). Today there remains a veil of ignorance covering the world, causing mankind to be fearful and misunderstand the character God.

This veil was put up in mercy to mankind, so that he would not be destroyed by the presence of God. This is why God told Moses, "Thou canst not see my face: for there shall no man see me, and live" (Exodus 33:20). The same word for "face" is translated as "presence" in Esther 1:10. God's desire is to prepare mankind to again dwell in His presence without being destroyed when that veil shall be removed at the second coming. The purpose of the gospel is to enable us to stand in His presence and not be consumed

The gospel is to bring about new life in us, a revival and reformation that will enable us to stand in the presence of God. The blueprint of this gospel plan is found in the sanctuary. This is why God said, "Let them make me a sanctuary; that I may dwell among them" (Exodus 25:8). The sanctuary itself consisted of three veils, one at the entrance of the outer court (Exodus 27:16; 38:18), another at the entrance to the holy place

(Exodus 26:33; 40:28), and the third at the entrance into the most holy place (Exodus 26:33). These veils represented man's separation from the presence of God.

We long for the time when there is nothing to separate us from God, either spiritually or physically. Two of these veils, the ones to the holy place and most holy place, hold great significance to Seventh-day Adventists. Understanding these two veils and their connection to revival will also help us to understand the coming revival of the latter rain, as well as give us the answer as to why this final revival tarries.

Revival and the First Opening

It is eye-opening to realize that every time a sanctuary veil was opened in the books of Daniel and Revelation, a major and powerful revival took place in connection with it. Consider, for example, the first opening, found in the book of Revelation.

> After this I looked, and, behold, a door was opened in heaven: and the first voice which I heard was as it were of a trumpet talking with me; which said, Come up hither, and I will shew thee things which must be hereafter. (Revelation 4:1)

John, in vision, was invited into the holy place of the sanctuary, the compartment into which Jesus entered after His resurrection and ascension. When Jesus died, the Bible records this fact: "Behold, the veil of the temple was rent in twain from the top to the bottom; and the earth did quake, and the rocks rent" (Matthew 27:51).

As Seventh-day Adventists, we understand that this rending or opening signified that the temple in heaven had taken the place of the one on earth, and that Jesus, after His resurrection, ascended to heaven to open the way to the heavenly holy place. It was on the day of Pentecost that the Holy Spirit was poured out on the disciples, signifying that Jesus was at the right hand of the Father and standing on their behalf in the holy place. The revival that ensued was closely connected with the opening of this veil. Mankind was then one step closer to God. Of this event, Ellen White penned:

> The rending of the veil of the temple showed that the Jewish sacrifices and ordinances would no longer be received. The great Sacrifice had been offered and had been accepted, and the Holy Spirit which descended on the day of Pentecost carried the minds of the disciples from the earthly sanctuary to the heavenly, where Jesus had entered by His own blood, to shed upon His disciples

the benefits of His atonement. But the Jews were left in total darkness. They lost all the light which they might have had upon the plan of salvation, and still trusted in their useless sacrifices and offerings. The heavenly sanctuary had taken the place of the earthly, yet they had no knowledge of the change. Therefore they could not be benefited by the mediation of Christ in the holy place. (*The Story of Redemption*, 386)

Two things are of key importance here. First, the opening of the veil was designed to carry the minds of the disciples from earthly things to heavenly things. Second, those who rejected the thought of the opening of the veil and continued to worship under the now useless system of sacrifices and offerings could not be benefited by Christ's mediation. The disciples learned of the heavenly opening after the fact. Had they heeded the seventy-week prophecy found in the ninth chapter of Daniel which foretold of Christ's ascension into the heavenly sanctuary, they would have been prepared for the event. But they suffered a great disappointment. Revival nonetheless took place in realization that Jesus was indeed in the heavenly realm, and in sweet anticipation they looked for the promise of the Spirit. As a result, revival swept the then-known world.

Revival and the Second Opening
The Bible prophesied of another major revival to come. This prophecy, found in Daniel 8:14, is foundational to Seventh-day Adventism. The seventy weeks looked forward to the opening of the veil to the holy place; the 2,300 days looked forward to opening of the veil to the most holy place, when Jesus entered to begin the work of the investigative judgment. In connection with this beginning work of judgment, Revelation 11:19 says:

And the temple of God was opened in heaven, and there was seen in his temple the ark of his testament: and there were lightnings, and voices, and thunderings, and an earthquake, and great hail.

This is the second opening of the temple found in the book of Revelation. Again, this opening of a veil brought with it a major revival (1840–44). However, like the first opening in A.D. 31, the people of God were again caught off guard. Like the disciples, they too learned in retrospect what had taken place in the realm of the unseen. They too suffered a great disappointment. They too had their minds on earthly things. The opening of the veil and the great revival that took place were to redirect their minds to heavenly things. Mankind was again one step closer to being face to face with God.

God had committed to His people a work to be accomplished on earth. The third angel's message was to be given, the minds of believers *were to be directed to the heavenly sanctuary,* where Christ had entered to make atonement of His people. (*Evangelism,* 695, emphasis added)

Like the first opening in A.D. 31, the second opening in 1844 brought about a worldwide revival. Like the unbelieving Jews, many denied that a heavenly transaction had taken place; that Jesus had entered into the most holy place to begin a work of judgment. Those who denied this came to constitute Babylon, the fallen churches, by refusing to have their minds directed to the most holy place.

The Third Opening and the Coming Revival

If the pattern is correct, and a third major revival is to take place as many Adventists hope for, we should find a third opening to take place that will bring with it this final revival. Revelation 15 describes the temple being opened a third and final time.

I looked, and, behold, the temple of the tabernacle of the testimony in heaven was opened: and the seven angels came out of the temple, having the seven plagues, clothed in pure and white linen, and having their breasts girded with golden girdles. (Revelation 15:5, 6)

On the Day of Atonement, there were two times that the veil to the most holy place was opened, which carried major significance. The first was the high priest's entrance into the holy of holies, the second was his departure to bless the waiting ones. The second opening (1844) was Christ's entry into the most holy, the third opening will be His exit from the most holy to return to this earth to meet His people face to face.

Could it be that the third and final revival to come revolves around God's people having an understanding concerning this third opening? Unequivocally yes! This third and final revival will prepare a people to see the face of God and live. However, there is a major difference between this final opening and the previous two.

The people of first and second openings could afford to understand *in hindsight* what had really taken place. They could afford to experience a great disappointment and rebound from it. Those who live in the time of the third opening cannot afford to make the same mistake, for probation will close with the third opening, which also signals the return of Jesus. There is no opportunity to learn anything in hindsight after the third opening.

The first and second openings were strikes one and two. We cannot afford to strike out on the final opening. The final revival must come *before* the third opening as a result of a confident expectation and anticipation of the outpouring of the Holy Spirit and the return of Christ—as confident as if we had an actual date, though we do not.

What a challenge! Our Adventist history reminds us of the great disappointment of 1844. To preach that Jesus is coming again with the same urgency as did our forefathers, presents a psychological barrier for many of us. Do we want another bitter experience, another great disappointment? Yet our zeal and urgency must surpass that of 1844, not based upon math, *but in faith that the Bridegroom is indeed about to come.*

The world must be warned that the veil in the temple is about to open for the last time. God's law will be seen by all humanity. It will be too late for those who reject the final warning given to world in the loud cry. Those who fail to experience this final revival will be left, attempting to hide themselves from the "presence" or "face" of the Lord God" to no avail.

Said the prophet:

> The clouds sweep back, and the starry heavens are seen, unspeakably glorious in contrast with the black and angry firmament on either side. The glory of the celestial city streams from the gates ajar. Then there appears against the sky a hand holding two tables of stone folded together. Says the prophet: "The heavens shall declare His righteousness; for God is judge himself." Psalm 50:6. That holy law, God's righteousness, that amid thunder and flame was proclaimed from Sinai as the guide of life, is now revealed to men as the rule of judgment. The hand opens the tables, and there are seen the precepts of the Decalogue, traced as with a pen of fire. The words are so plain that all can read them. Memory is aroused, the darkness of superstition and heresy is swept from every mind, and God's ten words, brief, comprehensive, and authoritative, are presented to the view of all the inhabitants of the earth.

> It is impossible to describe the horror and despair of those who have trampled upon God's holy requirements. The Lord gave them his law; they might have compared their characters with it, and learned their defects while there was yet opportunity for repentance and reform; but in order to secure the favor of the world, they set aside its precepts and taught others to transgress. They have endeavored to compel God's people to profane His Sabbath. Now they are condemned by that law which they have

despised. With awful distinctness they see that they are without excuse. (*The Great Controversy*, 639, 640)

Like the Jews in Christ's time who could not benefit from 'His mediatorial work, those who fail to experience the final revival in anticipation of the third opening will come up to that event unprepared, ultimately unable to benefit from Christ's work in the heavenly sanctuary. They will be left in total darkness. This then becomes our burden to preach the commandments of God and the righteousness of Christ by faith to His people in Babylon. We are to call them to revival and reformation, to prepare them to see God face to face, and to look into His law (character) without being condemned.

What is the sign that the third opening is upon us? How can we truly be revived knowing that Jesus is about to come and that He is about to pour out His Spirit upon His church to prepare them to give the loud cry and finish the work? The answer may be a surprise.

The sign of the first opening given to the disciples was the seventy-week prophecy. They were caught completely off guard, but they rebounded. The sign of the second opening given to the people of the various denominations in the mid 1800s was the 2,300-day prophecy. They saw it in advance, and this is what sparked the great revival. But we have a dilemma. There are no more time prophecies, and no more dates to set. So what then is the sign that will tell us in advance that all we have ever spoken of and taught is about to come to pass? Could it be that we are waiting for a sign when there is none?

Could it be that God is the One who is waiting for a *sign from us* so that He can open the temple for the third time and come again? What is that sign? The Bible tells us in these plain words:

> If I shut up heaven that there be no rain, or if I command the locusts to devour the land, or if I send pestilence among my people; if my people, which are called by my name, shall humble themselves, and pray, and seek my face, and turn from their wicked ways; then will I hear from heaven, and will forgive their sin, and will heal their land. (2 Chronicles 7:13, 14)

Second Chronicles 7:14 must become to us what Daniel 8:14 was to the advent believers of 1844. God has been waiting for His people to humble themselves and pray. All the while we, His people, have been waiting for some sign from God to signal the final events.

Could it be that we as a people have been *waiting* for the promise of the latter rain all these years instead of earnestly *praying* for it? Could this be the hold-up? Many of us are waiting for a sign like the national Sunday law or some other calamitous event to happen to cause us to spring into action. What if Elijah simply waited for the drought instead of praying for it? What if he simply waited, looking for the sign, the small cloud, half the size of a man's hand, to bring the rain instead of praying for it? (See 1 Kings 18.) Have we as people become obsessed with looking for the coming clouds instead of praying for them?

God wants to send the rain to prepare us to give the loud cry, which will lighten the whole world with His glory so that He can open the temple the third time to come out and bless His waiting people. When this third opening takes place, Isaiah's vision will then come to pass:

> He will destroy in this mountain the face of the covering cast over all people, and the vail that is spread over all nations. He will swallow up death in victory; and the Lord GOD will wipe away tears from off all faces; and the rebuke of his people shall he take away from off all the earth: for the Lord hath spoken it. And it shall be said in that day, Lo, this is our God; we have waited for him, and he will save us: this is the Lord; we have waited for him, we will be glad and rejoice in his salvation. (Isaiah 25:7–9)

This veil symbolizes the veil of ignorance that covers the world, and ultimately the veil that separates the seen from the unseen, the presence of God from the presence of man. When this veil is removed, two worlds will collide, the seen and the unseen, the natural and supernatural. "'The face of the covering cast over all people, and the veil that is spread over all nations,' was finally to be destroyed. Isaiah 25:7. The Spirit of God was to be poured out upon all flesh" (*Prophets and Kings*, 371).

So before this opening, the minds of God's people must again be redirected from earthly pursuits to heavenly. Imagine the revival that would take place if we had a date and time for the second coming—but we do not. What we do have is God waiting for the sign, waiting for us to proclaim by faith, waiting for us to live and act like we really believe that Jesus is soon to come again, and waiting for His people to "call a solemn assembly" (Joel 1:14; 2:15).

The same zeal that animated the 1840–44 movement must again animate the people of God, and this without any sign but the sign of revival, reformation, and prayer. God is waiting for us to fall in line. The foolish virgins make the request, "Lord, Lord, open to us" (Matthew 25:11). But there will be no fourth opening. Probation is about to close, shutting the door of mercy for eternity. We must, by faith, warn the world that the veil is about to be opened for the third and final time.

One more point is of great interest to us. In both the first and the second openings, there was an incredible movement of prayer. The disciples wanted to make sure they were right with one another and with God in anticipation of some great event that was about to take place. Likewise, the people of the second opening, in anticipation of some great event, sought to put away their differences and make sure they were right with one another and with God.

The same must be done now but to a greater degree by the people of God in anticipation of some great event that has been prophesied to take place. May God hear our prayers and humble our hearts, causing us to unify. May we individually seek the daily baptism of the Holy Spirit that we may truly be prepared for that final opening.

Group Discussion Questions

1. Discuss the concept of being prepared for the third opening.

2. How does the final opening differ from the first two openings?

3. How does the preaching of the third opening relate to "faith"?

4. What impacted you most about this chapter?

Chapter 12
The Coming Midnight Cry

The parable of the ten virgins opens up with ten virgins going forth to meet the bridegroom. The timing and chronology of this parable is absolutely crucial in order to understand the coming "midnight cry" of the parable (Matthew 25:6). What is it that first caused the ten virgins to go "forth to meet the bridegroom"? Can we determine the time that they first went forth to meet Him?

First, the ten virgins (as opposed to the harlot of Babylon and her daughters) must have had information, or "light," that the bridegroom was coming. How would they have received this information but by the Word of God? "Thy word is a lamp unto my feet, and a light unto my path" (Psalm 119:105). The lamps in their possession at the opening of the parable pointed them to the realization that the Bridegroom was coming. In the book of Daniel, we find that special light is given in the time of the end.

> They that be wise shall shine as the brightness of the firmament; and they that turn many to righteousness as the stars for ever and ever. But thou, O Daniel, shut up the words, and seal the book, even to the time of the end: many shall run to and fro, and knowledge shall be increased. (Daniel 12:3, 4)

Sometime then, toward the time of the end (after 1798), knowledge would be increased, and this would cause those who heed it to "shine." The ten virgins all received this light intellectually. "The class represented by the foolish virgins are not hypocrites. They have a regard for the truth, they have advocated the truth, they are attracted to those who believe the truth" (*Christ's Object Lessons*, 408).

The parable of Matthew 25 has its explanation mostly in the vision of Zechariah 4. In the vision, the lamp is flanked by two olive trees. The angel explained this scene as "the two anointed ones, that stand by the Lord of the whole earth" (Zechariah 4:14). Ellen White explained it thus: "The anointed ones standing by the Lord of the whole earth have the position once given to Satan as covering cherub" (*The Review and Herald*, July 20, 1897). They are standing "by" or beside a lighted candle. The angel explained this candlestick as representing "the Lord of the whole earth." This vision clearly points to Christ standing between the cherubim in the most holy place. Christ entered the most holy place in 1844, and this is the light that caused the organized Christian church in the 1840s to begin to preach the message that Jesus was coming again and to prepare to go forth to meet Him.

We know then that the original "going forth" to meet the bridegroom has a specific application to the laying of the foundation for God's last-day church in the years leading up to and surrounding 1844. The excitement of Christ's soon coming caused the people of God to go forth preaching the three angels' messages with great zeal. In the mid to late 1800s the church exercised untiring efforts to reach the lost with the light they had been given. Many years passed, and the Lord tarried. We are now in that "tarrying time." The virgins have all fallen asleep.

While none should be sleeping, the sleep of the wise was one of disappointment. They desired the Lord to come and to come quickly. They labored under the guidance of the Spirit, yet were "asleep," not to their danger, but to the closeness of the event. In a sense, it was a sweet sleep as "the sleep of a labouring man is sweet" (Ecclesiastes 5:12).

The foolish, however, were asleep under a deception, asleep to their danger. "They were lulled to sleep by the cry of peace and safety, and did not keep their lamps trimmed and burning" (*That I May Know Him*, 215). Their sleep is sleep of indolence. Proverbs describes the difference between the ant and sluggard that is reminiscent of the characters of the wise and foolish virgins.

> Go to the ant, thou sluggard; consider her ways, and be wise: which having no guide, overseer, or ruler, provideth her meat in the summer, and gathereth her food in the harvest. How long wilt thou sleep, O sluggard? when wilt thou arise out of thy sleep? Yet a little sleep, a little slumber, a little folding of the hands to sleep: so shall thy poverty come as one that travelleth, and thy want as an armed man. (Proverbs 6:6–11)

The *wise* ant gathered her food beforehand so that she had enough in the time of need. Therefore, when the wise ant did sleep, it was sweet. She knew she had enough. The foolish slept and slumbered, ignorant of the great crisis ahead and unprepared for it. Like the armed man in want, if they could have, they would have robbed the five wise of their oil.

So what woke up the sleeping virgins? It was a midnight cry. Midnight is the time when we are most likely to be in our deepest sleep. Just as the virgins had originally gone forth to the meet the bridegroom, a result of the study of God's Word, so a revival in the study of God's Word will reveal that the midnight cry will be given only when we wake up to give it. "With mighty power the cry is *again* to be sounded in our large centers of population. 'Behold the Bridegroom cometh, go ye out to meet Him'" (*Pamphlet 20*, 4, emphasis supplied).

> This gospel of the kingdom shall be preached in all the world for a witness unto all nations; and then shall the end come. (Matthew 24:14)

> The third angel's message is to be sounded *by God's people*. It is to swell to the loud cry. The Lord has a time appointed when He will bind off the work; but when is that time?—*when the truth proclaimed for these last days shall go forth as a witness to all nations, then shall the end come.* If the power of Satan can come into the very temple of God and manipulate things as he pleases, *the time of preparation will be prolonged.* (*Manuscript Releases*, vol. 9, 212, emphasis added)

> It is the privilege of every Christian not only to look for *but to hasten the coming of our Lord Jesus Christ*, (2 Peter 3:12, margin). Were all who profess His name bearing fruit to His glory, how quickly the whole world would be sown with the seed of the gospel. Quickly the last great harvest would be ripened, and Christ would come to gather the precious grain. (*Christ's Object Lessons*, 69, emphasis added)

The five wise virgins received light from the Word of God, and they were to herald His coming with urgency as if they had an exact date for His coming, even though they had none. They arose and trimmed their lamps, determined to give a straight testimony to the world. This light that burns brighter will enlighten the whole world with the glory of God. The foolish also awakened, but with great suspicion.

> There is to be in the [Seventh-day Adventist] churches *a wonderful manifestation of the power of God, but it will not move upon those who have not humbled themselves before the Lord*, and opened the door of the heart by confession and repentance. In the manifestation of that power *which lightens the earth with the glory of God*, they will see only something which in their blindness they think dangerous, something which *will arouse their fears*, and they will brace themselves to resist it. Because the Lord does not work according to their ideas and expectations they will

oppose the work. "Why," they say, "should we not know the Spirit of God, when we have been in the work so many years? (*Last Day Events*, 209, emphasis added)

The third angel's message will not be comprehended, *the light which will lighten the earth with its glory will be called a false light*, by those who refuse to walk in its advancing glory. (*The Review and Herald*, May 27, 1890, emphasis added)

Speaking to this point, the Bible says, "Woe unto them that call evil good, and good evil; that put darkness for light, and light for darkness; that put bitter for sweet, and sweet for bitter! Woe unto them that are wise in their own eyes, and prudent in their own sight! Isaiah 5:20, 21. Men in responsible positions, who appear to be defenders of the truth, will have blocked the work of the loud cry.

The time and care and labor required to counteract the influence of those who have worked against the truth has been a terrible loss; for we might have been years ahead in spiritual knowledge; and many, many souls might have been added to the church if those who ought to have walked in the light had followed on to know the Lord, that they might know His going forth is prepared as the morning. But when so much labor has to be expended right in the church to counteract the influence of workers who have stood as a granite wall against the truth God sends to His people, *the world is left in comparative darkness.*

But in many, many places, and on many, many occasions it could truthfully be said as in Christ's day of those who profess to be God's people, that not many mighty works could be done, because of their unbelief. Many who have been bound in fetters of darkness have been respected because God has used them, and their unbelief has aroused doubt and prejudice *against the message of truth which angels of heaven were seeking to communicate through human agencies*—justification by faith, the righteousness of Christ. (*Manuscript Releases*, vol. 14, 110, 111)

This may be specifically pointing to the work of the five foolish virgins. Remember that the "angels of heaven" "seeking to communicate through human agencies" are described as the "two anointed ones" in Zechariah's vision.

The mission of the two anointed ones is to communicate light and power to God's people. It is to receive blessing for us that they stand in God's presence. As the olive trees empty themselves into the golden pipes, so the heavenly messengers seek to communicate all that they receive from God. The whole heavenly treasure awaits our demand and reception; and as we receive the blessing, we in our turn are to impart it. Thus it is that the holy lamps are fed, and the church becomes a light bearer in the world. (*Testimonies to Ministers and Gospel Workers*, 510)

The foolish virgins fought against the light and oil being communicated through God's angels to his people. They fought against the loud cry. They fought the idea of aggressively moving forward. They fought going up to take possession of the land as did the ten spies in the time of Joshua. They fought against the giving of so straight a testimony, so bright a light.

The five foolish braced themselves against the concentrated light of the five wise, the same glory that is to fill the whole earth. They believed this would bring on an unwarranted time of trouble. This straight testimony, which is a testimony being given to the world is a rebuke against the lukewarmness of Laodicean members and will bring about a shaking.

I asked the meaning of the shaking I had seen and was shown that it would be caused by the straight testimony called forth by the counsel of the True Witness to the Laodiceans. This will have its effect upon the heart of the receiver, and will lead him to exalt the standard and pour forth the straight truth. Some will not bear this straight testimony. They will *rise up against it*, and this is what will cause a shaking among God's people.

I saw that the testimony of the True Witness has not been half heeded. The solemn testimony upon which the destiny of the church hangs has been lightly esteemed, if not entirely disregarded. This testimony must work deep repentance; all who truly receive it will obey it, and be purified. …

The numbers of this company had lessened. Some had been shaken out and left by the way. [Yes, the five foolish virgins arose too, but it was only self and against the light.] The careless and indifferent, who did not join with those who prized victory and salvation enough to perseveringly plead and agonize for it, did not obtain it, and *they were left behind in darkness*, and their places were immediately filled by others taking hold of the truth and coming into the ranks. Evil angels still pressed around them, but could have no power over them.

> *I heard those clothed with the armor speak forth the truth with great power. It had effect.* Many had been bound; some wives by their husbands, and some children by their parents. The honest who had been prevented from hearing the truth now eagerly laid hold upon it. All fear of their relatives was gone, and the truth alone was exalted to them. *They had been hungering and thirsting for truth; it was dearer and more precious than life. I asked what had made this great change. An angel answered, "It is the latter rain, the refreshing from the presence of the Lord, the loud cry of the third angel."* (*Early Writings*, 270, 271, emphasis supplied)

The message of light of the five wise virgins was not directed to the five foolish but rather to those genuinely seeking light. "For Zion's sake will I not hold my peace, and for Jerusalem's sake I will not rest, until the righteousness thereof go forth as brightness, and the salvation thereof as *a lamp that burneth. And the Gentiles shall see thy righteousness, and all kings thy glory*: and thou shalt be called by a new name, which the mouth of the Lord shall name" (Isaiah 62:1,2, emphasis added). The burning lamps of the five wise virgins were directed to the Gentiles, those who are in the error of darkness. This *burning lamp*, spoken of in Isaiah 62, Ellen White equates to the loud cry given by the five wise virgins.

> The salvation of God will go forth from you as a *lamp that burneth*. If your own hearts are filled with light from above, wherever you may be you will shed light upon others. He will bless you in your service, and you will see of His salvation.

> The third angel was seen flying in the midst of heaven, heralding the commandments of God and the faith of Jesus. The message loses none of its power in its onward flight. John saw the work increasing until the whole earth was filled with the glory of God. With intensified zeal and energy we are to carry forward the work of the Lord till the close of time. (*Counsels to Parents, Teachers, and Students*, 548, emphasis added)

> Oh, how I long to see church members clothed with their beautiful garments, and prepared *to go forth to meet the Bridegroom!* Many are expecting to sit down to the marriage supper of the

Lamb, who are unprepared for the coming of the King. They are like the blind; they do not seem to discern their danger.

The Lord calls upon you, oh, church that has been blessed with the truth, to give a knowledge of this truth to those who know it not. From one end of the world to the other must the message of Christ's soon coming be proclaimed. The third angel's message—the last message of mercy to a perishing world—is so precious, so glorious. Let the truth go forth as a lamp that burneth. Mysteries into which angels desire to look, which prophets and kings and righteous men desired to know, the church of God is to make known. (*Medical Ministry*, 333, 334, emphasis added)

This "burning lamp" should have been going forth since 1888, but it was opposed.

God meant that the watchmen should arise and with united voices send forth a decided message, giving the trumpet a certain sound, that the people might all spring to their post of duty and act their part in the great work. Then the strong, clear light of that other angel who comes down from heaven having great power, would have filled the earth with his glory. We are years behind; and those who stood in blindness and hindered the advancement of the very message that God meant should go forth from the *Minneapolis meeting as a lamp that burneth*, have need to humble their hearts before God and see and understand how the work has been hindered by their blindness of mind and hardness of heart.

Hours have been spent in quibbling over little things; golden opportunities have been wasted while *heavenly messengers have grieved, impatient at the delay*. (*Manuscript Releases*, vol. 14, 111, emphasis added)

This lamp that "burneth" not only sheds light on God's character but also on the character of the harlot woman, Babylon. "For the commandment is a lamp; and the law is light; and reproofs of instruction are the way of life: *to keep thee from the evil woman, from the flattery of the tongue of a strange woman*" (Proverbs 6:23, 24, emphasis added).

The strange woman who flatters, according to the book of Revelation, is "Mystery Babylon" (Revelation 17:5, 6). Her "flattery" is toward those who disregard the law of God. In Daniel 11:32, Mystery Babylon is under the symbol of the king of the north. There is says: "Such as do wickedly against the covenant shall he (the king of the north, Mystery Babylon) corrupt by flatteries: but the people that do know their God shall be strong, and do exploits."

In an unfortunate chain of events, the foolish virgins will join the opposition in seeking to extinguish the light and the "exploits" of the five wise virgins. Thus, while the harlot Babylon speaks with a flattering tongue, the five wise virgins will be empowered to speak forth under the influence of the Holy Spirit. Like the early church, they too will speak with "tongues of fire," or tongues "on fire."

Ellen White wrote, "I am instructed to say that when the Holy Spirit gives tongue and utterance, we shall see a work done similar to that done on the day of Pentecost. The representatives of Christ will work intelligently" (*Australasian Union Conference Record*, March 11, 1907). The wise will be blessed with the gift of burning tongues, although this time in zeal rather than in languages. Like Jeremiah, they will say, "His word was in mine heart as a burning fire shut up in my bones, and I was weary with forbearing, and I could not stay" (Jeremiah 20:9).

Nevertheless, the foolish will oppose it. Yes, "many a star that we have admired for its brilliance will then go out in darkness" (*Prophets and Kings*, 188).

> Men whom He has greatly honored will, in the closing scenes of this earth's history, pattern after ancient Israel. … A departure from the great principles Christ has laid down in His teachings, a working out of human projects, using the Scriptures to justify a wrong course of action under the perverse working of Lucifer, will confirm men in misunderstanding, and the truth that they need to keep them from wrong practices will leak out of the soul like water from a leaky vessel. (*Manuscript Releases*, vol. 13, 379, 381)

> Many will show that they are not one with Christ, that they are not dead to the world, that they may live with him; *and frequent will be the apostasies of men who have occupied responsible positions.* (*The Review and Herald*, September 11, 1888)

The five foolish virgins attempted to trim their lamps, but nothing happened. No light. They realized too late that the work they refused to engage in was the work of the Lord. In refusing to engage in the harvest, they realized that they rejected the light, explaining why their light had gone out. They rejected the oil, the latter rain outpouring of the Holy Spirit.

Just as the oil ceased to flow when the last empty vessel was filled in the story of Elisha and the widow (2 Kings 4:1–6), so the oil will cease to flow when the last open person hears the truth and accepts it. It is at this time when the preaching work is finished when the light of the lamps of the wise have enlightened all who will be enlightened, when the foolish will realize what they have done. Like the ten spies, and all who listened to them, they discover that they will not enter the Promised Land; they will perish in the wilderness of this earth (see Jeremiah 4:26). In a desperate attempt, they go to get oil to engage in the work, but it will be too late.

> When the third angel's message closes, mercy no longer pleads for the guilty inhabitants of the earth. The people of God have accomplished their work. ... Then Jesus ceases his intercession in the sanctuary above. He lifts his hands, and with a loud voice says, "It is done;" and all the angelic host lay off their crowns as he makes the solemn announcement: "He that is unjust, let him be unjust still; and he which is filthy, let him be filthy still; and he that is righteous, let him be righteous still; and he that is holy, let him be holy still." Revelation 22:11. Every case has been decided for life or death. Christ has made the atonement for his people, and blotted out their sins. The number of his subjects is made up; "the kingdom and dominion, and the greatness of the kingdom under the whole heaven," is about to be given to the heirs of salvation, and Jesus is to reign as King of kings, and Lord of lords. *When he leaves the sanctuary, darkness covers the inhabitants of the earth.* ... The wicked have passed the boundary of their probation; the Spirit of God, persistently resisted, *has been at last withdrawn.* (*The Great Controversy*, 1888 ed., 613, emphasis supplied)

> Then I saw Jesus lay off His priestly attire and clothe Himself with His most kingly robes. Upon His head were many crowns, a crown within a crown. Surrounded by the angelic host, He left heaven. The plagues were falling upon the inhabitants of the earth. Some were denouncing God and cursing Him. *Others rushed to the people of God and begged to be taught how they might escape His judgments. But the saints had nothing for them. The last tear for sinners had been shed, the last agonizing prayer offered, the last burden borne, the last warning given. The sweet voice of mercy was no more to invite them. When the saints, and all heaven, were interested for their salvation, they had no interest for themselves. Life and death had been set before them. Many desired life, but made no effort to obtain it. They did not choose*

life, and now there was no atoning blood to cleanse the guilty, no compassionate Saviour to plead for them, and cry, "Spare, spare the sinner a little longer." All heaven had united with Jesus, as they heard the fearful words, "It is done. It is finished." The plan of salvation had been accomplished, but few had chosen to accept it. And as mercy's sweet voice died away, fear and horror seized the wicked. With terrible distinctness they heard the words, "Too late! too late!"

Those who had not prized God's Word were hurrying to and fro, wandering from sea to sea, and from the north to the east, to seek the Word of the Lord. Said the angel, "They shall not find it. There is a famine in the land; not a famine of bread, nor a thirst for water, but for hearing the words of the Lord. What would they not give for one word of approval from God! but no, they must hunger and thirst on. Day after day have they slighted salvation, prizing earthly riches and earthly pleasure higher than any heavenly treasure or inducement. They have rejected Jesus and despised His saints. The filthy must remain filthy forever." (*Early Writings*, 281, 282, emphasis added)

Group Discussion Questions

1. What parallel impacted you the most from this chapter?

2. What are some of the modern-day wilderness luxuries that cause the church to fear crossing the Jordan?

3. What do you think needs to happen for the church members to realize their individual responsibility for revival and the advancement of the church locally and globally?

4. What needs to happen for the church to understand the need for united movement?

Chapter 13
The Coming Nor'easter

A recent whether phenomenon has been taking the forecasting world by storm. Called a nor'easter (combining the words "north" and "east"), this storm is created by a combination of conditions coming from the north and the east, affecting adversely the eastern coastline of the United States.

While the news of a coming nor'easter is almost never welcomed, the Bible speaks of a coming "nor'easter" that will result in the harvest of thousands of souls and trouble for one entity in particular—Babylon. "But tidings out of the east and out of the north shall trouble him: therefore he shall go forth with great fury to destroy, and utterly to make away with many" (Daniel 11:44). In order to understand this, let us take a deeper look at the verses surrounding this Scripture.

Daniel 11:40–45 Chronology

The clearest presentation of the timing of the latter rain is found in Daniel 11:40–45. After quoting the Scripture, including Daniel 12:1, a brief overview of these verses follows:

• **11:40**—At the time of the end shall the king of the south push at him: and the king of the north shall come against him like a whirlwind, with chariots, and with horsemen, and with many ships; and he shall enter into the countries, and shall overflow and pass over.

• **11:41**—He shall enter also into the glorious land, and many countries shall be overthrown: but these shall escape out of his hand, even Edom, and Moab, and the chief of the children of Ammon.

• **11:42**—He shall stretch forth his hand also upon the countries: and the land of Egypt shall not escape.

• **11:43**—But he shall have power over the treasures of gold and of silver, and over all the precious things of Egypt: and the Libyans and the Ethiopians shall be at his steps.

• **11:44**—But tidings out of the east and out of the north shall trouble him: therefore he shall go forth with great fury to destroy, and utterly to make away many.

• **11:45**—He shall plant the tabernacles of his palace between the seas in the glorious holy mountain; yet he shall come to his end, and none shall help him.

- **12:1**—At that time shall Michael stand up, the great prince which standeth for the children of thy people: and there shall be a time of trouble, such as never was since there was a nation even to that same time: and at that time thy people shall be delivered, every one that shall be found written in the book.

- **Verse 40**: *The time of the end:* The "time of the end" had its beginning in the period between 1798 and 1844, when the book of Daniel was to be unsealed and understood.

> He said, Go thy way, Daniel: for the words are closed up and sealed *till the time of the end.* Many shall be purified, and made white, and tried; but the wicked shall do wickedly: and none of the wicked shall understand; but the wise shall understand." Remember, the parable of the ten virgins has its beginning in this time period, for this is when *light* from Daniel *began to shine*, that the bridegroom was about to come. (Daniel 12:9, 10, emphasis added)

Ellen White wrote of the coming of Christ, relating that the book of Daniel had been unsealed in 1798.

> The apostle Paul warned the church not to look for the coming of Christ in his day. "That day shall not come," he says, "except there come a falling away first, and that man of sin be revealed." 2 Thessalonians 2:3. Not till after the great apostasy, and the long period of the reign of the "man of sin," can we look for the advent of our Lord. The "man of sin," which is also called "the mystery of iniquity," "the son of perdition," and "that wicked," represents the papacy, which, as foretold in prophecy, was to maintain its supremacy for 1260 years. This period ended in 1798. The coming of Christ could not take place before that time. Paul covers with his caution the whole of the Christian dispensation down to the year 1798. *It is this side of that time that the message of Christ's second coming is to be proclaimed.*
> No such message has ever been given in past ages. Paul, as we have seen, did not preach it; he pointed his brethren into the then far-distant future for the coming of the Lord. The Reformers did not proclaim it. Martin Luther placed the judgment about three hundred years in the future from his day. But since 1798 the book

of Daniel has been unsealed, knowledge of the prophecies has increased, and many have proclaimed the solemn message of the
judgment near. (*The Great Controversy*, 356, emphasis added)

The kings of the north and south: These two kings represent various
powers that rose and fell throughout the reigns of Medo-Persia, Greece,
Rome, and papal Rome. A few indicators help us to identify the king of
the north in the latter verses of Daniel 11. Speaking of this king, Daniel 11
points out that "arms shall stand on his part, and they shall pollute the
sanctuary of strength, and shall take away the daily sacrifice, and they
shall place the abomination that maketh desolate" (verse 31). This was
fulfilled by the papacy as it polluted the teachings of the heavenly sanctuary, setting up and earthly temple its place during the 1,260 years of papal
dominion that lasted from A.D. 538 to 1798.

Verse 32 states, "Such as do wickedly against the covenant shall he
corrupt by flatteries." The papacy bribed and corrupted many into turning against the covenant of God.

Daniel 11:33 refers to the persecution by the papacy during the Dark
Ages. "They that understand among the people shall instruct many:
yet they shall fall by the sword, and by flame, by captivity, and by spoil,
many days."

The king shall do according to his will; and he shall exalt himself,
and magnify himself above every god, and shall speak marvel-
lous things against the God of gods, and shall prosper till the
indignation be accomplished. ... Neither shall he regard the God
of his fathers, nor the desire of women, nor regard any god: for
he shall magnify himself above all. (Daniel 11:36, 37)

These verses apply to the papacy as well, especially Paul's description
of the papacy when he wrote, "Let no man deceive you by any means:
for that day shall not come, except there come a falling away first, and
that man of sin be revealed, the son of perdition; who opposeth and ex-
alteth himself above all that is called God, or that is worshipped; so that
he as God sitteth in the temple of God, shewing himself that he is God"
(2 Thessalonians 2:3, 4).

The king of the south, on the other hand, is in an opposite location
from the king of the north, and he symbolizes an equal, yet opposite, evil.
The king of the south rose out of the Grecian empire after the death of
Alexander the great. Ptolemy, one of Alexander's four generals took the
southern part of his kingdom, of which Egypt was the most prominent. So
the king of the south symbolizes Egypt, but we're going to look even deeper.

"At the time of the end shall the king of the south push at him" (Daniel 11:40); that is, push at, or war against, the king of the north. The clue to finding out the identity of the king of the south is to be found in the term "the time of the end," a period referring to the 1798 completion of the 1,260-day prophecy. It is at this time that the papacy (king of the north) received a deadly wound from an aggressor. Discover the aggressor, and there you have the king of the south. Again, from the pen of inspiration we read concerning the fall of the papacy in 1798:

> The periods here mentioned—"forty and two months," and "a thousand two hundred and threescore days"—are the same, alike representing the time in which the church of Christ was to suffer oppression from Rome. The 1260 years of papal supremacy began with the establishment of the papacy in A.D. 538, and would therefore terminate in 1798. At that time a French army entered Rome, and made the pope a prisoner, and he died in exile. …

> "When they shall have finished [are finishing] their testimony." The period when the two witnesses were to prophesy clothed in sackcloth ended in 1798. As they were approaching the termination of their work in obscurity, war was to be made upon them by the power represented as "the beast that ascendeth out of the bottomless pit." In many of the nations of Europe the powers that ruled in Church and State had for centuries been controlled by Satan, through the medium of the papacy. But here is brought to view a new manifestation of satanic power. (*The Great Controversy*, 266, 268)

The "beast from the bottomless pit" is the same power as the "king of the south" who attacks the papacy at the time of the end. It "rises" from the symbolic south. Continuing, she wrote:

> It had been Rome's policy, under a profession of reverence for the Bible, to keep it locked up in an unknown tongue, and hidden away from the people. Under her rule the witnesses prophesied, "clothed in sackcloth." But another power—the beast from the bottomless pit—was to arise to make open, avowed war upon the word of God.

> "The great city" in whose streets the witnesses are slain, and where their dead bodies lie, is "spiritually" Egypt. Of all nations

presented in Bible history, Egypt most boldly denied the existence of the living God, and resisted his commands. No monarch ever ventured upon more open and high-handed rebellion against the authority of Heaven than did the king of Egypt. When the message was brought him by Moses, in the name of the Lord, Pharaoh proudly answered, "Who is Jehovah, that I should obey his voice to let Israel go? I know not Jehovah, neither will I let Israel go." Exodus 5:2 ... This is atheism; and the nation represented by Egypt would give voice to a similar denial of the claims of the living God, and would manifest a like spirit of unbelief and defiance. The "great city" is also compared, "spiritually," to Sodom. The corruption of Sodom in breaking the law of God was especially manifested in licentiousness. And this sin was also to be a pre-eminent characteristic of the nation that should fulfill the specifications of this scripture.

According to the words of the prophet, then, a little before the year 1798 some power of satanic origin and character would rise to make war upon the Bible. And in the land where the testimony of God's two witnesses should thus be silenced, there would be manifest the atheism of the Pharaoh, and the licentiousness of Sodom.

This prophecy has received a most exact and striking fulfillment in the history of France. (*The Great Controversy*, 269)

The king of the south represents atheism. It was this power that "pushed against" the papacy at the time of the end.

All too well the people had learned the lessons of cruelty and torture which Rome had so diligently taught. A day of retribution at last had come. It was not now the disciples of Jesus that were thrust into dungeons and dragged to the stake. Long ago these had perished or been driven into exile. Unsparing Rome now felt the deadly power of those whom she had trained to delight in deeds of blood. "The example of persecution which the clergy of France had exhibited for so many ages, was now retorted upon them with signal vigor. The scaffolds ran red with the blood of the priests. The galleys and the prisons, once crowded with Huguenots, were now filled with their persecutors. Chained to the bench and toiling at the oar, the Roman Catholic clergy experienced all those woes which their church had so freely inflicted on the gentle heretics. (*The Great Controversy*, 283)

The latter part of verse 40, speaks of the papacy, the king of the north, overthrowing the king of the south. This is simply stating that the papacy comes back into strength and overthrows the king of the south, represented by atheism and secularism. This overthrow of "atheism," began with the 1989 fall of communistic and atheistic Russia when the papacy, along with the United States, helped bring about its fall. Since then, atheism and apostate Christianity have been in a heated battle, which can especially be seen in the political landscape of the United States. Atheism and secularism wage war against the Christian right, but in the end it will be overcome by the Christian right aided by the miracle-working power of Satan.

• **Verse 41–43**: these verses speak of the growing influence the papacy would have in the world after it began to regain its strength. It would continue to gain strength, wielding it over the nations of the world. We are now living in this time.

• **Verse 44:** This brings us to verse 44, the pivotal verse, for it is verse 44 that brings about the time of trouble through these tidings from the north and the east. Without verse 44, nothing else can move forward! We will come to back that shortly. Notice though, what happens as a result of verse 44.

• **Verse 45:** Here, the planting of his tabernacles is synonymous with the setting up of the abomination of desolation that is also described in 2 Thessalonians 2:1–4, in which the man of sin is said to sit in the temple of God "showing himself that he is God." This is ultimately fulfilled in the passing of the Sunday law. His "tabernacle" represents his counterfeit system of God's plan of salvation, which is found in the true tabernacle in heaven. "Thy way, O God, is in the sanctuary" (Psalm 77:13). Thus, when the king of the north (the papacy) plants his tabernacle (or establishes his false system of worship, of which Sunday worship is the symbol) in the midst of the seas (in the midst of "peoples, nations, multitudes, and tongues"), it will be the equivalent to that which is found in Revelation 13:16, 17: "He causeth all, both small and great, rich and poor, free and bond, to receive a mark in their right hand, or in their foreheads: and that no man might buy or sell, save he that had the mark, or the name of the beast, or the number of his name." It is in this way that he will "go forth with great fury to destroy, and utterly to make away many" (Daniel 11:44).

Jesus referred to the "abomination of desolation" (Matthew 24:15) and pointed to the Roman armies surrounding Jerusalem to destroy it. So when spiritual Rome surrounds spiritual Israel with the intent to destroy it, we may know that the abomination has been set up. Ellen White told us that this "setting up" is the enforcement of the Sunday law. "As the siege of Jerusalem by the Roman armies was the signal for flight to the Judean Christians, so the assumption of power on the part of our nation in the decree enforcing the papal sabbath will be a warning to us" (*Testimonies for the Church*, vol. 5, 464). Then follows Daniel 12:1.

• **Daniel 12:1**: Michael stands up; probation closes; the great time of trouble begins that includes the seven last plagues of Revelation 16 (see *The Great Controversy*, 613–634).

Back to verse 44—what are these "tidings" out of the north and the east that so infuriate the Papacy, that in response, she attempts to pass a Sunday law coupled with a death decree? It is none other than the preaching under the latter rain. The Sabbath or sealing message is said to come from the east (see Exodus 31:13–17; Revelation 7:1–4). This is part of the message of three angels in Revelation 14:6–12. The fourth angel's message comes from the symbolic north (see Revelation 18:1–4). It is the combination of these messages that troubles the papacy and sets off the time of trouble. No message, no trouble!

God's people have been preaching the three angel's messages for more than 160 years, and it has not yet angered Babylon. Why? It is because it will not be preached with papacy-angering power until the angel of Revelation 18 (coming "down" from the symbolic north) *lighting the earth* with its glory and merges with the three angels' messages that the "nor'easter" will be created that troubles Babylon. This fourth angel is to add "power" and "glory" to the three angels' messages.

As Seventh-day Adventists, it is important for us to understand that without these glad "tidings" Babylon will never be "troubled." *The time of trouble is to begin first for Babylon* with the tidings from the north and the east, the latter rain, and loud cry. In response to the tidings of this powerful "nor'easter," Babylon answers by setting off a time of trouble *against the people of God* through legislation of Sunday observance to counter the glory that lightens the earth. But this time of trouble will be short lived, for in Daniel 12:1, we read that Michael (Jesus Christ) will stand up to deliver His people, "and there shall be a time of trouble such as never was." Babylon will then be in *serious trouble* because of her sins reaching unto heaven and her attack against the people of God. Powerful thought! The "glad tidings" for the seeking soul, the light that lays open the sins of Babylon will be seen as "troubling news" by the king of the north and all who support him.

So mark this point: *the papacy is not being troubled today.* Why? No nor'easter! The people of God are still asleep to the fact that God is waiting on us to bring the storm, the great outpouring of oil. All the players have taken their place on the field of action, *but the people of God. They are waiting on us. Angels are waiting on us.* The winds of strife cannot be loosed until the people of God have accomplished the work of verse 44 (see Revelation 7:1–4.)

The Almost Nor'easter of 1888

In 1831, a message began to brew (ironically?) in the *northeastern* states of America. William Miller began to preach based on Daniel 8:14. These tidings grew with great momentum, and became what we know today as the three angels' messages. These messages picked up further power and velocity. In the city of Minneapolis in 1888, the foretold nor'easter was beginning to brew in order to add force and power to three angels' messages. The "glad tidings" began to be preached, coupled with the three angels' messages. But it "troubled" some of whom the Lord did not intend for it to trouble. Opposition arose, and the storm that was intended to trouble the papacy was temporarily held at bay. Today that storm may be beginning to brew again. Will we be ready to allow it to gain the vital momentum needed to do its work?

Group Discussion Questions

1. Discuss the three angels' messages. What are they? (See Revelation 14:6–14.)

2. Why is it important to understand that we are not waiting for the time of trouble, but rather that the time of trouble is waiting for us?

3. How can a faulty understanding of our mission delay the second coming?

4. What impacted you most about this chapter?

Chapter 14
Waiting for a Crisis?

As Seventh-day Adventists, we have looked forward to the time when a Sunday law will be enacted against the people of God. Many have eagerly been awaiting this event to catapult us into the final scenes of earth's history. Therefore, the Sunday law is seen as the sign that the latter rain will fall. Any talk of the latter rain falling before then is seen by some as out of order. Hence, the thought is we must wait until the Sunday law takes place, which will bring about a shaking in God's church before God will pour out the latter rain on a purified people.

So pause for a moment. What if this were not true? What if the latter rain precedes the Sunday law? What are the implications? In this chapter we will examine the evidence and will find out the truth as to why it is crucial to understand that the latter rain does indeed begin *before* the laws enforcing Sunday observance and prohibiting Sabbath observance are enacted.

Latter Rain—A Season, Not a Day

First, it is important to understand that the early rain was a season, not a day. The initial outpouring, or the early rain, took place in Acts 2, but there was another second major outpouring in Acts 4 as well. The fact is that the early rain fell many times during that season (see Acts 8:14–17; 9:17; 10:44–47; 11:15; 13:52; 19:1–7). Zechariah 10:1 speaks of "showers" to come, not a shower. Notice that Ellen White described Pentecost as a "season."

> John says, "I saw another angel come down from heaven, having great power; and the earth was lightened with his glory." Then, as at the Pentecostal season, the people will hear the truth spoken to them, every man in his own tongue. (*The Review and Herald*, July 20, 1886)

The key questions for us are these: when does the season begin? Does it begin before or after the Sunday law? The answers are that the season begins before the Sunday law, and it will fall after the Sunday law as well. The latter rain is a season, not a day. Therefore, we may expect numerous outpourings of the Spirit of God in various places on Planet Earth over a short period of time.

Latter Rain Season Began in 1888

Next, we may well ask: are we now in that season, or is the season yet to come? We are told that in 1888, a most precious message came to the church through Elders Jones and Waggoner. That message was, to a noticeable degree, resisted.

> An unwillingness to yield up preconceived opinions, and to accept this truth, lay at the foundation of a large share of the opposition manifested at Minneapolis against the Lord's message through Brethren {E. J.} Waggoner and {A. T.} Jones. By exciting that opposition Satan succeeded in shutting away from our people, in a great measure, *the special power of the Holy Spirit that God longed to impart to them.* The enemy prevented them from obtaining that efficiency which might have been theirs in carrying the truth to the world, as the apostles proclaimed it after the day of Pentecost. The light that is to lighten the whole earth with its glory *was resisted*, and by the action of our own brethren has been in a great degree kept away from the world. (*Selected Messages*, Book 1, 234, 235, emphasis added)

> The time is right upon us when the whole earth will be lightened with His glory. That light is beginning to shine already. (*Manuscript Releases*, 357)

> The time of test is just upon us, for the loud cry of the third angel *has already begun* in the revelation of the righteousness of Christ, the sin-pardoning Redeemer. *This is the beginning of the light of the angel whose glory shall fill the whole earth.* For it is the work of every one to whom the message of warning has come, to lift up Jesus, to present Him to the world as revealed in types, as shadowed in symbols, as manifested in the revelations of the prophets, as unveiled in the lessons given to His disciples and in the wonderful miracles wrought for the sons of men. Search the Scriptures; for they are they that testify of him. (*The Review and Herald*, November 22, 1892, emphasis added)

Notice that Ellen White declared this to be the latter rain at a time when there was no enforcement of a Sunday law. The latter rain season was ready to begin; in fact, it had "already begun" but was halted, *not because of the failure of Sunday laws to be enforced* but because of the people's unpreparedness/unwillingness to accept the message. It is evident here that had Ellen White believed that a Sunday law was needed before the outpouring of the latter rain, she would never have made this statement knowing that the events were supposedly out of order as no Sunday law enforcement had yet been passed. Thus, if the enforcement of the Sunday law was not needed for God to begin to pour out "that light," which "is to lighten the whole earth with its glory" upon the church in 1888, why would one be needed now?

The Chronology of Daniel 11:40–45 and the Spirit of Prophecy

In the previous chapter, we studied the chronology of Daniel 11:40–45 and saw that verse 44 was the pivotal verse that moves this earth from a time of peace and safety into a time of trouble. We saw the tidings of the gospel, empowered by the Holy Spirit, will infuriate the papacy and cause it to move to destroy any who receive these tidings. Notice how Ellen White follows Daniel's chain of events that produced the latter rain, which will anger the papacy. This results in the passing of a Sunday law to destroy the people of God.

> The power attending the message will only madden those who oppose it. ... The church appeals to the strong arm of civil power, and in this work, papists and Protestants unite. As the movement for Sunday enforcement becomes *more bold and decided*, the law will be invoked against commandment keepers. (*The Review and Herald*, April 27, 1911, emphasis added)

This describes perfectly Daniel 11:44, 45. So what will happen after the death decree is invoked? Daniel 12:1 follows in perfect order. Note the following.

> I heard those clothed with the armor speak forth the truth with great power. It had effect. ... I asked what had made this great change. An angel answered, "It is the latter rain, the refreshing from the presence of the Lord, the loud cry of the third angel."
> Great power was with these chosen ones. Said the angel, "Look ye!" My attention was turned to the wicked, or unbelievers. They were all astir. *The zeal and power with the people of God had aroused and enraged them.* Confusion, confusion, was on every side. *I saw measures taken against the company who had the light and power of God.* ...
>
> Soon I heard the voice of God, which shook the heavens and the earth. There was a mighty earthquake. (*Early Writings*, 271, 272, emphasis added)

Again, notice that they spoke forth the truth with power as a result of the latter rain. This is what enraged the wicked. Measures (Sunday law, death decree) were taken against them. Then God's voice is heard—a perfect description of Daniel 11:44–12:1.

> I saw that God had children who do not see and keep the Sabbath. They have not rejected the light upon it. And at the commencement of the time of trouble, we were filled with the Holy Ghost as we went forth and proclaimed the Sabbath more fully. This enraged the churches and nominal Adventists, as they could not refute the Sabbath truth. And at this time God's chosen all saw clearly that we had the truth, and they came out and endured the persecution. (*Early Writings*, 33, 34)

What enraged the wicked? It was the preaching of the Sabbath more fully, the tidings of the cross in connection with the three angels' messages.

Babylon Fallen

Some suggest that when the angel of Revelation 18 descends with the message "Babylon is fallen," that she must already be considered "fallen," meaning she has already passed a Sunday law; thus, the final message cannot go forward until the Sunday law is passed. Since this angel represents the latter rain, the Sunday law must come first for the angel's proclamation to have any truth and power to it. Such statements as these are used:

> "She made all nations drink of the wine of the wrath of her fornication." Revelation 14:6–8. How is this done? By forcing men to accept a spurious sabbath. (*Testimonies for the Church*, vol. 8, 94) Not yet, however, can it be said that ... "she made *all nations* drink of the wine of the wrath of her fornication." She has not yet made all nations do this. ...

> Not until this condition shall be reached, and the union of the church with the world shall be fully accomplished throughout Christendom, will the fall of Babylon be complete. The change is a progressive one, and the perfect fulfillment of Revelation 14:8 is yet future. (*The Great Controversy*, 389, 390)

> When do her sins reach unto heaven? When the law of God is finally made void by legislation. (*The Signs of the Times*, June 12, 1893)

The key to this dilemma is quite simple and very logical. The fact is that this angel descends to add power not only the second angel of Revelation 14 whose message is that "Babylon is fallen" (Revelation 14:8), but it also adds power to the first and third angels' messages as well.

> The three angels' messages are to be combined, giving their threefold light to the world. In the Revelation, John says, "I saw another angel come down from heaven, having great power; and the earth was lightened with his glory." … *This represents the giving of the last and threefold message of warning to the world.* (*Maranatha*, 173, emphasis added)

God never violates His mode of operation. Before people can be condemned, they must first have had light that they have rejected. "This is the condemnation, that light is come into the world, and men loved darkness rather than light, because their deeds were evil" (John 3:19).

The angel of Revelation 18 descends with "light." Therefore, we learn that it is the rejection of this light that forces the angel to declare that "Babylon is fallen."

> Thousands upon thousands will listen who have never heard words like these. In amazement they hear the testimony that Babylon is the church, fallen because of her errors and sins, *because of her rejection of the truth sent to her from Heaven.* (*The Great Controversy*, 1888 ed., 606, 607, emphasis added)

What is this "truth" sent to Babylon from heaven that she rejects and thus is declared to be fallen? It is the tidings from the east and the north, the loud cry of the message of Christ's righteousness in relation to the law and the Sabbath. The angel first adds power to the first angel's message, which is the law of God in connection with the cross of Christ.

We go forth, not first preaching Babylon is fallen, but rather the Sabbath "more fully." The messages must be given in their order. The rejection of this message will then lead to the fall of Babylon just in the same way it did in 1844.

Again, a perfect picture of Daniel 11:44, 45. We go forth first, declaring the Sabbath more fully. In response, the churches are enraged, which is followed by an intentional Sunday law. The rejection of the preaching of the Sabbath "more fully" by the passing of Sunday law in defiance of the "light sent from heaven" then adds power to the second angel's message: "Babylon is fallen." The passing of the Sunday law only serves to add force to the message that it could not have had previously because it will be seen that God's people indeed spoke about events that came to pass. Only when Babylon is fallen, can the third angel's warning against receiving the mark have 'its best effect. Babylon's rejection of this three-fold message is what causes her to fall. When she falls, or sets up, the very next event is Michael standing up, not the loud cry. Probation has closed.

Daniel, Chapters 1 through 3, Lays Out the Order of Events

It is interesting to note that the order of events is typified in the first three chapters of Daniel. In Daniel 1, the story is told of the four Hebrews who received a ten-day testing time over their faithfulness to God. As a result of their faithfulness, they were given wisdom and understanding by God.

In Daniel 2, the king of Babylon had a dream of the future that he could not remember or understand. But Daniel and his friends, who had received of the Spirit of God, were able to show him the prophetic truths of the future.

Daniel 3 showed a direct contradiction to the message given with power. Here, an image was set up, which represented a counterfeit of the genuine Word of God given to the king of Babylon. The command was given to bow down before this image, and the faithful Hebrews Hannaniah [Shadrach], Mishael [Meshach], and Azariah [Abednego] refused. A death decree ensued, but they were delivered.

In like manner, God's people must experience Pentecostal power. They will then be given ability to "dream dreams" and "see visions" (Joel 2:28). They will boldly speak the truth of the Sabbath. In direct contradiction to this message, Babylon will set up an "image" to which all are to bow down—a counterfeit Sabbath. Refusal to do so will bring about a death decree, but Jesus will save his people out of the fires. They shall not have to taste death. Preaching with power will come first, and this is what will anger Babylon to retaliate by setting up the counterfeit Sabbath law—as in the type, so in the antitype.

It interesting to remember that the decree given by Medo-Persia to have no one pray to any God for 30 days was passed intentionally, albeit secretly against Daniel. So in the type, the Sunday law will point at the people of God to rid them from earth because of the power of their preaching under the influence of the Holy Spirit.

Is Now the Time of the Latter Rain or Not?

This issue becomes quite simple. Some say we should not be praying for the latter rain, nor expect it to fall now because now is not the time for the latter rain. The Sunday law has not yet been passed.

Contrary to this theory, Ellen White wrote:

Let us, with contrite hearts, pray most earnestly that now, in the time of the latter rain, the showers of grace may fall upon us. At every meeting we attend, our prayers should ascend that at this very time, God will impart warmth and moisture to our souls. As we seek God for the Holy Spirit, it will work in us meekness, humbleness of mind, a conscious dependence upon God for the perfecting latter rain. If we pray for the blessing in faith, we shall receive it as God has promised. (*The Review and Herald*, March 2, 1897, emphasis added)

"Now" is not the time of the Sunday law, but "now" is the time of the latter rain. So which comes first? Remember the parable of ten virgins found in Matthew 25. Five were wise, five foolish. The foolish ones decided to wait for a signal, a sign, a crisis before seeking oil (Spirit) to fill their vessels. The wise were filled before the crisis hit. Let us be preparing now, ready now, pleading now to be filled with the latter rain, so that when the Sunday law crisis hits, we will be found ready—not wanting.

In the next chapter, we look at this quote used to teach that the Sunday law will supposedly come before the latter rain: "The great issue so near at hand [enforcement of Sunday laws] will weed out those whom God has not appointed and He will have a pure, true, sanctified ministry prepared for the latter rain" (*Selected Messages*, Book 3, 385).

Remember, the rainy season has already begun—before the Sunday law—and it will continue after the Sunday law is in place just up to the close of probation. As in the early rain, the people who came under its influence received of its power; this is also so under the latter rain. As people come into the faith, they too will be filled with the latter-rain power to preach and be fitted for translation, for all who are saved will need the latter-rain power in the last days. While the Sunday law will cause a shaking, and even prepare the church for a special outpouring, we will see in the next chapter, just what outpouring this is, and why it is not the initial outpouring of the latter rain that began in 1888.

Group Discussion Questions

1. Why is it dangerous to wait for the Sunday law before preparing for the crisis?

2. How does this concept reveal the foolishness of the foolish virgins?

3. What impacted you most about this chapter?

4. How can you as an individual, and we as a church, wake others to our need to advance?

5. Discuss the concept of the rainy seasons. Does the latter rain come before or after the Sunday law? Why?

Chapter 15
Ellen White's Plain Chronology of These Events

In this chapter, we will examine from one source: Ellen White's testimony, which shows that the latter rain falls at least twice. The latter rain falls both *before* and *after* Sunday laws. Remember that the early rain fell twice of major significance in the books Acts. Once before the time of persecution for the church (Acts 2), the second time after persecution had begun (Acts 4). The main point in this chapter is that it is faulty to say the latter rain is poured out only after, or only before, the Sunday law. It is both pre and post, which will be shown clearly.

Let us look at Ellen White's testimony in its entirety. Look out for the two times the people of God will be "lighted up" with God's glory. One is before the measures taken against them take place (Sunday law), and the other is as the wicked are preparing to carry out the death decree just prior to Christ coming on the clouds of heaven. One opens the rainy season; the other seals up, or closes, the rainy season.

The Shaking

> I saw some, with strong faith and agonizing cries, pleading with God. Their countenances were pale, and marked with deep anxiety, expressive of their internal struggle. Firmness and great earnestness was expressed in their countenances; large drops of perspiration fell from their foreheads. Now and then their faces would light up with the marks of God's approbation, and again the same solemn, earnest, anxious look would settle upon them.

> Evil angels crowded around, pressing darkness upon them to shut out Jesus from their view, that their eyes might be drawn to the darkness that surrounded them, and thus they be led to distrust God, and murmur against Him. Their only safety was in keeping their eyes directed upward. Angels of God had charge over His people, and as the poisonous atmosphere of evil angels was pressed around these anxious ones, the heavenly angels were continually wafting their wings over them to scatter the thick darkness.

As the praying ones continued their earnest cries, at times a ray of light from Jesus came to them, to encourage their hearts, and light up their countenances. Some, I saw, did not participate in this work of agonizing and pleading. They seemed indifferent and careless. They were not resisting the darkness around them, and it shut them in like a thick cloud. The angels of God left these, and went to the aid of the earnest, praying ones. I saw angels of God hasten to the assistance of all who were struggling with all their power to resist the evil angels, and trying to help themselves by calling upon God with perseverance. But His angels left those who made no effort to help themselves, and I lost sight of them. (*Early Writings*, 269, 270)

The struggle here is not with men, but with angels. It is an internal conflict, not an external one. No mention of a Sunday law or persecution from Babylon is mentioned as the reason for this struggle.

I asked the meaning of the shaking I had seen, and was shown that it would be caused by the straight testimony called forth by the counsel of the True Witness to the Laodiceans. This will have its effect upon the heart of the receiver, and will lead him to exalt the standard and pour forth the straight truth. Some will not bear this straight testimony. They will rise up against it, and this is what will cause a shaking among God's people.

I saw that the testimony of the True Witness has not been half heeded. The solemn testimony upon which the destiny of the church hangs has been lightly esteemed, if not entirely disregarded. This testimony must work deep repentance; all who truly receive it will obey it, and be purified. (*Early Writings*, 270)

It is the straight testimony that had caused such internal struggle in the people of God. Those who obey are purified and prepared for the latter rain. This shaking is not caused by a Sunday law, but by the straight testimony. Ellen White told us that the shaking had commenced as early as 1850, and it is still going on today. "The mighty shaking has commenced, and will go on, and all will be shaken out who are not willing to take a hold and unyielding stand for the truth, and sacrifice for God and his cause" (*The Present Truth*, April 1, 1850). This shaking is an invisible one. A person may be shaken out of the church yet still have his name on the books and attend every Sabbath.

Said the angel, "List ye!" Soon I heard a voice like many musical instruments all sounding in perfect strains, sweet and harmonious. It surpassed any music I had ever heard, seeming to be full of mercy, compassion, and elevating, holy joy. It thrilled through my whole being. Said the angel, "Look ye!" My attention was then turned to the company I had seen, who were mightily shaken. I was shown those whom I had before seen weeping and praying in agony of spirit. The company of guardian angels around them had been doubled, and they were clothed with an armor from their head to their feet. They moved in exact order, like a company of soldiers. Their countenances expressed the severe conflict which they had endured, the agonizing struggle they had passed through. Yet their features, marked with severe internal anguish, now shone with the light and glory of heaven. They had obtained the victory, and it called forth from them the deepest gratitude, and holy, sacred joy. (*Early Writings*, 270, 271)

This is not victory over the beast as that is yet to come in this vision. This victory denotes victory over self, gained through confession of sin and much pleading. The five wise virgins awakened. Their lamps were trimmed, and through much prayer and weeping, they were revitalized and prepared with oil and light to go forth with sacred joy. But as we will see, they would soon face another battle.

The numbers of this company had lessened. Some had been shaken out and left by the way. The careless and indifferent, who did not join with those who prized victory and salvation enough to perseveringly plead and agonize for it, did not obtain it, and they were left behind in darkness, and their places were immediately filled by others taking hold of the truth and coming into the ranks. Evil angels still pressed around them, but could have no power over them.

I heard those clothed with the armor speak forth the truth with great power. It had effect. Many had been bound; some wives by their husbands, and some children by their parents. The honest who had been prevented from hearing the truth now eagerly laid hold upon it. All fear of their relatives was gone, and the truth alone was exalted to them. They had been hungering and thirsting for truth; it was dearer and more precious than life. I asked what had made this great change. An angel answered, "It is the latter rain, the refreshing from the presence of the Lord, the loud cry of the third angel. (*Early Writings*, 271)

The five wise virgins had preaching the midnight cry, the loud cry. The foolish virgins' lights had gone out. The five wise had victory over their besetments and self, and this qualified them to receive the latter rain. This was the opening of the rainy season. If we are correct that Ellen White follows the pattern of Daniel, we should next expect a mention of preaching with power followed by persecution, and indeed we see that as she continued:

> Great power was with these chosen ones. Said the angel, "Look ye!" My attention was turned to the wicked, or unbelievers. They were all astir. The zeal and power with the people of God had aroused and enraged them. Confusion, confusion, was on every side. I saw measures taken against the company who had the light and power of God. (*Early Writings*, 272)

Measures are thus taken against those who had the light, the burning lamps. *Maranatha*, page 188, refers to these "measures" as being the Sunday law.

> In the last conflict the Sabbath will be the special point of controversy throughout all Christendom. Secular rulers and religious leaders will unite to enforce the observance of the Sunday; and as milder measures fail, the most oppressive laws will be enacted. It will be urged that the few who stand in opposition to an institution of the church and a law of the land ought not to be tolerated. (*Maranatha*, 188)

Clearly, they had already received the latter rain. The measures that were taken were as a result of the five wise preaching with great power. The rainy season, as far as Ellen White was concerned, in agreement with Daniel, began before the "measures taken against" the people of God.

> Darkness thickened around them, yet they stood firm, approved of God, and trusting in Him. I saw them perplexed; next I heard them crying unto God earnestly. Day and night their cry ceased not: "Thy will, O God, be done! If it can glorify Thy name, make a way of escape for Thy people! Deliver us from the heathen around about us. They have appointed us unto death; but Thine arm can bring salvation." These are all the words which I can

bring to mind. All seemed to have a deep sense of their unworthiness, and manifested entire submission to the will of God; yet like Jacob, every one, without an exception, was earnestly pleading and wrestling for deliverance.

Soon after they had commenced their earnest cry, the angels, in sympathy, desired to go to their deliverance. But a tall, commanding angel suffered them not. He said: "The will of God is not yet fulfilled. They must drink of the cup. They must be baptized with the baptism." (*Early Writings*, 272)

Here, after they received the latter rain started to preach, they were thrust into a new conflict, not only one of internal struggle, but this time one with external enemies. They were again pleading, but they needed to receive another baptism.

Soon I heard the voice of God, which shook the heavens and the earth. There was a mighty earthquake. Buildings were shaken down on every side. I then heard a triumphant shout of victory, loud, musical, and clear. I looked upon the company who, a short time before, were in such distress and bondage. Their captivity was turned. *A glorious light shone upon them. How beautiful they then looked!* All marks of care and weariness were gone, and health and beauty were seen in every countenance. Their enemies, the heathen around them, fell like dead men; they could not endure the light that shone upon the delivered, holy ones. This light and glory remained upon them, until Jesus was seen in the clouds of heaven, and the faithful, tried company were changed in a moment, in the twinkling of an eye, from glory to glory. And the graves were opened, and the saints came forth, clothed with immortality, crying, "Victory over death and the grave;" and together with the living saints they were caught up to meet their Lord in the air, while rich, musical shouts of glory and victory were upon every immortal tongue. (*Early Writings*, 272, 273, emphasis added)

Here is the sealing up, or finishing, of the rainy season. After probation has closed, the people of God will again be given a glorious outpouring, this time to prepare them, not to give the loud cry, but to stand in the presence of Jesus.

It could not be clearer that the latter rain falls *before* the "measures" taken against the people of God. The latter rain falls before the Sunday law, preparing us to give the loud cry, but it also falls after the Sunday law at the close of the rainy season, preparing us to stand in the presence of God.

Putting It All Together

The straight testimony produces a shaking that has been going on since 1850, which will ultimately lead to the fitting up for the loud cry. Those shaken out by the straight testimony may remain in the church, but they will not discern the falling away of the spirit. They will not realize that they have no oil reserves. Those who do receive the latter rain will go out to give the loud cry at the commencement of the time of trouble—not when Michael stands up, for at that time probation closes for everyone, and there is no purpose in preaching.

> At the commencement of the time of trouble, we were filled with the Holy Ghost as we went forth and proclaimed the Sabbath more fully. This enraged the churches and nominal Adventists, as they could not refute the Sabbath truth. And at this time God's chosen all saw clearly that we had the truth, and they came out and endured the persecution. (*Christian Experience and Teachings of Ellen G. White*, 93)

The latter rain will be given at the beginning of the time of trouble to empower the three angels' messages. This, in turn, will enrage the churches just like in Daniel's testimony. The Sunday law will be passed *in response* to the power of the message. This Sunday law will "weed out" those who miss the latter rain for the loud cry, yet they will remain within the church physically. All the while others will come in from Babylon to take their places. God will then have a "purified church" to receive the "sealing" latter rain, which will prepare them for translation.

In this light, this sentence may be rightly understood: "The great issue [enforcement of Sunday laws] so near at hand will weed out those whom God has not appointed and He will have a pure, true, sanctified ministry prepared for the latter rain" (*Selected Messages*, Book 3, 385). This would be for the "sealing" latter rain, which will prepare a people to stand in God's presence after the close of probation, not for the "loud cry" latter rain that will empower a people to give the final message of mercy with power.

The seal of God, or the "sealing latter" rain, serves to preserve us through the seven last plagues. It will be given to those who refuse the mark and stand firm. It will be received after the "loud cry" of the latter rain, which is a separate outpouring that prepares us to give the loud cry. Both are identified as the latter rain; yet, both are two distinct events.

At that time the "latter rain," or refreshing from the presence of the Lord, will come, to give power to the loud voice of the third angel, and prepare the saints to stand in the period when the seven last plagues shall be poured out. (*Early Writings*, 85).

Thus, the latter rain will be given before the time of trouble to give the loud cry. It will be given to those coming into the faith who take the place of the five foolish virgins, it will be presented again near the end of the time of trouble just before the close of probation to seal the people of God prepare them to go through the plagues and stand in the presence of God. They will stand fast in the face of the beast, so they will be kept safely during the plagues and fitted for translation.

It is the latter rain which revives and strengthens them to pass through the time of trouble. (*The Review and Herald*, May 27, 1862)

God's people pray. The loud cry latter rain is given. They begin to preach a straight testimony. Those who do not receive the loud cry of the latter rain think this straight preaching will bring on trouble. They see something they think is dangerous. They rise up against it but remain in the church. At the same time, the glory of the message infuriates the other churches because they are losing their members by the thousands to the preaching of the truth. Persecution ensues through Sunday laws. This is the physical shaking that weeds out those who had not received the loud cry of the latter rain.

Those who stand against the Sunday law death decree are sealed. Those who did not receive the latter rain to take part in the loud cry, leave the church in the face of physical danger. Multitudes, will come in to take their places, receiving the baptism of the Spirit. The church is thus "weeded out," leaving a purified people who receive the "sealing" latter rain that serves to "revive and strengthen" them to keep them through the time when the four winds are loosed and probation closes. This sealed number will enter heaven.

When the third angel's message closes, mercy no longer pleads for the guilty inhabitants of the earth. The people of God have accomplished their work. They have received "the latter rain," "the refreshing from the presence of the Lord," and they are prepared for the trying hour before them. Angels are hastening to and fro in Heaven. An angel returning from the earth announces that his work is done; the final test has been brought upon the world, and all who have proved themselves loyal to the divine precepts have received "the seal of the living God." ... Then Jesus ceases his intercession in the sanctuary above. He lifts his hands, and with a loud voice says, "It is done;" and all the angelic host lay off their crowns as he makes the solemn announcement: "He that is unjust, let him be unjust still; and he which is filthy, let him be filthy still; and he that is righteous, let him be righteous still; and he that is holy, let him be holy still. (*The Great Controversy*, 1888 ed., 613)

Again, this shows that the latter rain both precedes and succeeds the Sunday law. One in the form of power for the loud cry, opening the rainy season *before* the mark of the beast (Daniel 11:44), the other in the form of the "sealing" latter rain, closing the rainy season and also reviving and preparing God's people for the time when Michael stands up in Daniel 12:1, closing probation. They will shine like the stars (Daniel 12:3). In other words, they are the five wise virgins whose lights have not burned out.

As stated earlier, the early rain was twice given monumental significance in the book of Acts. The first time the disciples were under no threat whatsoever by the churches of the day. However, the "power attending the message" changed all that. Persecution followed. In Acts 4, we find this moving prayer:

• **Acts 4:29**: And now, Lord, behold their threatenings: and grant unto thy servants, that with all boldness they may speak thy word,

• **Acts 4:30**: By stretching forth thine hand to heal; and that signs and wonders may be done by the name of thy holy child Jesus.

• **Acts 4:31**: And when they had prayed, the place was shaken where they were assembled together; and they were all filled with the Holy Ghost, and they spake the Word of God with boldness.

Of these verses Ellen White commented:

The disciples prayed that greater strength might be imparted to them in the work of the ministry; for they saw that they would meet the same determined opposition that Christ had encountered when upon the earth. While their united prayers were ascending in faith to heaven, the answer came. The place where they were assembled was shaken, and they were endowed anew with the Holy Spirit. Their hearts filled with courage, they again went forth to proclaim the Word of God in Jerusalem. "With great power gave the apostles witness of the resurrection of the Lord Jesus," and God marvelously blessed their efforts. (*The Acts of the Apostles*, 67)

Could it be that the disciples needed an extra boost to preach in face of heated opposition? Could it be that after we begin to preach the first angel's message with power, proclaiming the glad tidings that trouble the king of the north, that we might see these words of the messenger of the Lord fulfilled? "Yet when the storm of opposition and reproach bursts upon them, some, overwhelmed with consternation, will be ready to exclaim: 'Had we foreseen the consequences of our words, we would have held our peace.'" ... Then, feeling their utter helplessness, they flee to the Mighty One for strength (*The Great Controversy*, 608).

Is it not clear that these things are a consequence of our words (Daniel 11:44)? God will empower His people "anew" like He did the disciples to declare Babylon fallen (Daniel 11:45) and to be fitted for translation (Daniel 12:1, 3).

Group Discussion Questions

1. Discuss the order of events and why it is critical to understand.

2. Why is the church not suffering persecution?

3. What is the difference between the beginning of the rainy season, and the ending of the rainy season?

4. What impacted you most in this chapter?

Chapter 16
Chain Reactions

I n the twentieth chapter of the book of Revelation, an angel with a chain in his hand prepares to bind the devil for a thousand years (Revelation 20: 1–3). The understanding is that Satan is not bound by a literal chain, but by a chain of circumstances. The wicked are dead, and the righteous are in heaven as they were caught up by Christ's second appearing, leaving Satan with no one to tempt. He is bound on earth awaiting his final destruction. What is it that leads to this binding? Could there be a chain of events, a chain reaction that leads to the chaining of the devil? If so, what is it that sets off this chain reaction?

The following is an outline of the order of events that will inevitably lead to his destruction, and the mechanism that sets off this reaction.

Global Repentance and Prayer Leads to Global Rain

On the day of Pentecost, the church gathered together to pray. They were all in one place and of one accord. As a result, the Spirit was poured out in that "one place." From that "one-place" outpouring, the entire then-known world was turned upside down by relatively few people. The latter rain in contrast to a "one-place" event is a "global" one. The whole world is to be lightened with the glory of the angel of Revelation 18:1–3. It would make sense, then, that if the latter rain were poured out globally, there would be many people, praying in many places at one time, upon which that rain will fall. We are promised:

If I shut up heaven that there be no rain, or if I command the lo-custs to devour the land, or if I send pestilence among my people; If my people, which are called by my name, shall humble them-selves, and pray, and seek my face, and turn from their wicked ways; then will I hear from heaven, and will forgive their sin, and will heal their land. (2 Chronicles 7:13, 14)

Blow the trumpet in Zion, sanctify a fast, call a solemn assembly. (Joel 2:15)

We are told to call a solemn assembly to gather as a people to pray for the outpouring of the latter rain. Ellen White saw the following in vision:

In visions of the night representations passed before me of a great reformatory movement among God's people. Many were praising God. The sick were healed and other miracles were wrought. A spirit of intercession was seen, even as was manifested before the great day of Pentecost. ... I heard voices of thanksgiving and praise, and there seemed to be a reformation such as we witnessed in 1844. (*Counsels on Health*, 580)

This global movement of prayer for revival and reformation will bring about a global lighting of the earth with the glory of God. This movement will parallel the momentum of 1844.

Global Rain Leads to a Global Cry

This global outpouring leads to a global empowering of the three angels' messages.

They that be wise shall shine as the brightness of the firmament; and they that turn many to righteousness as the stars for ever and ever. (Daniel 12:3)

I saw jets of light shining from cities and villages, and from the high places and the low places of the earth. God's Word was obeyed, and as a result there were memorials for Him in every city and village. His truth was proclaimed throughout the world. (*Testimonies for the Church*, vol. 9, 28, 29)

Hundreds and thousands were seen visiting families, and opening before them the Word of God. Hearts were convicted by the power of the Holy Spirit, and a spirit of genuine conversion was manifest. On every side doors were thrown open to the proclamation of the truth. The world seemed to be lightened with the heavenly influence. (*Testimonies for the Church*, vol. 9, 126)

It is obvious that many voices saying the same thing is louder than only a few. The loud cry is loud because it will be given all over the earth simultaneously. No longer will God's people leave the work of evangelism to our few powerful, Spirit-filled, leading evangelists. In thousands of villages, towns, and cities across the globe, men and women filled with the fire of God will turn their hometowns upside down. The earth will be lightened with the glory of God. It is then that the gospel will truly go to "every nation, and kindred, and tongue, and people" (Revelation 14:6).

Global Cry Leads to Global Exodus

"I heard another voice from heaven, saying, Come out of her, my people, that ye be not partakers of her sins, and that ye receive not of her plagues" (Revelation 18:4). This global loud cry leads to an incredible and unprecedented exodus, a global exodus out of Babylon.

> As the time comes for it [the message of the third angel] to be given with greatest power, the Lord will work through humble instruments, leading the minds of those who consecrate themselves to His service. The laborers will be qualified rather by the unction of His Spirit than by the training of literary institutions. Men of faith and prayer will be constrained to go forth with holy zeal, declaring the words which God gives them. The sins of Babylon will be laid open. The fearful results of enforcing the observances of the church by civil authority, the inroads of Spiritualism, the stealthy but rapid progress of the papal power,—all will be unmasked. By these solemn warnings the people will be stirred. Thousands upon thousands will listen who have never heard words like these. (*The Great Controversy*, 1888 ed., 606)

> Servants of God, endowed with power from on high with their faces lighted up, and shining with holy consecration, went forth to proclaim the message from heaven. Souls that were scattered all through the religious bodies answered to the call, and the precious were hurried out of the doomed churches, as Lot was hurried out of Sodom before her destruction. (*Early Writings*, 279)

> Many ... will be seen hurrying hither and thither, constrained by the Spirit of God to bring the light to others. The truth, the Word of God, is as a fire in their bones, filling them with a burning desire to enlighten those who sit in darkness. ... Multitudes will receive the faith and join the armies of the Lord. (*The Review and Herald*, July 23, 1895)

In every religious body on planet earth, people will hear the truth and come out of the various false systems. However, this global exodus will produce a negative global effect.

Global Exodus Leads to Global Attention and Persecution

The Exodus enraged Pharaoh and brought about his attempt to wipe out Israel. The religious leaders in the days of the apostles began to persecute the early church as a result of its Pentecostal power to draw away their own adherents. So it will be in the final days.

As the religious bodies of the world, Christian and non-Christian, begin to lose their adherents, it will stir up a global curiosity that will lead to a global spirit of strife. As Babylon is suffering this incredible loss of souls, "one post shall run to meet another, and one messenger to meet another, to shew the king of Babylon that his city is taken at one end" (Jeremiah 51:31). They will trace the source of this sudden disruption to one comparatively tiny group of people. This will turn the focus of the world upon Seventh-day Adventists. Ellen White wrote:

> The apostle Paul declares that "all that will live godly in Christ Jesus shall suffer persecution." 2 Timothy 3:12. Why is it, then, that persecution seems in a great degree to slumber? The only reason is that the church has conformed to the world's standard, and therefore awakens no opposition. The religion which is current in our day is not of the pure and holy character that marked the Christian faith in the days of Christ and His apostles. It is only because of the spirit of compromise with sin, because the great truths of the Word of God are so indifferently regarded, because there is so little vital godliness in the church, that Christianity is apparently so popular with the world. Let there be a revival of the faith and power of the early church, and the spirit of persecution will be revived, and the fires of persecution will be rekindled. (*The Great Controversy*, 48, emphasis added)

This global exodus brings about a global rekindling of persecution in response. We are again given the reason in the following statement:

> In amazement they hear the testimony that Babylon is the church, fallen because of her errors and sins, because of her rejection of the truth sent to her from Heaven. As the people go to their former teachers with the eager inquiry, Are these things so? the ministers present fables, prophesy smooth things, to soothe their fears and quiet the awakened conscience. But since many refuse to be satisfied with the mere authority of men and demand a plain "Thus saith the Lord," the popular ministry, like the Pharisees of old, filled with anger as their authority is questioned, will denounce the message as of Satan and stir up the sin-loving multitudes to revile and persecute those who proclaim it. (*The Great Controversy*, 1888 ed., 606, 607, emphasis added)

So then, the final persecution comes in response to the loud cry, not the other way around. This is why persecution lingers. God's people arouse none because we yet lack the power of the Spirit, Pentecostal power, latter-rain power. As God's people awaken, lay aside their differences, humble themselves in seeking revival and reformation by the early rain experience, and then come together to seek the Lord for the latter rain, His Spirit is poured out. This lighting of the world will cause a global exodus, leading to a universal reaction of hatred.

> As the controversy extends into new fields and the minds of the people are called to God's downtrodden law, Satan is astir. The power attending the message will only madden those who oppose it. The clergy will put forth almost superhuman efforts to shut away the light lest it should shine upon their flocks. By every means at their command they will endeavor to suppress the discussion of these vital questions. The church appeals to the strong arm of civil power, and, in this work, papists and Protestants unite. As the movement for Sunday enforcement becomes more bold and decided, the law will be invoked against commandment keepers. (*The Great Controversy*, 607)

The Sunday law will be passed in response to the loud cCry, not the other way around. Could this be why we seem to be waiting for a Sunday law that at best seems very distant? As the law against prayer to any god was instituted purposely and specifically against Daniel the prophet (see Daniel 6), so the law of Sunday sacredness will be instituted in response to, purposefully, and specifically, against an empowered Seventh-day Adventist church that has aroused the wrath of the world and religionists by preaching a message so powerful that it robs them of their adherents.

> When the protection of human laws shall be withdrawn from those who honor the law of God, there will be, in different lands, a simultaneous movement for their destruction. As the time appointed in the decree draws near, the people will conspire to root out the hated sect. It will be determined to strike in one night a decisive blow, which shall utterly silence the voice of dissent and reproof. (*The Great Controversy*, 635)

Simultaneously, in response to the global movement of God's people, Satan initiates his own plot to destroy this global mission. His global plot to destroy the people of God will be thwarted by that chain-bearing angel of Revelation, chapter 20.

Global Persecution Leads to Global Rescue

> After these things I saw four angels standing on the four corners of the earth, holding the four winds of the earth, that the wind should not blow on the earth, nor on the sea, nor on any tree. And I saw another angel ascending from the east, having the seal of the living God: and he cried with a loud voice to the four angels, to whom it was given to hurt the earth and the sea, Saying, Hurt not the earth, neither the sea, nor the trees, till we have sealed the servants of our God in their foreheads. (Revelation 7:1–3)

When persecution breaks out, and the death decree is given, the four winds are let loose, probation closes, the temple in heaven is opened (see Revelation 15) the third and final time. This will be in preparation for the plagues to be poured out, and Jesus will come to deliver His people from their great time of trouble.

Wrote the prophet Daniel: "At that time shall Michael stand up, the great prince which standeth for the children of thy people: and there shall be a time of trouble, such as never was since there was a nation even to that same time: and at that time thy people shall be delivered, every one that shall be found written in the book" (Daniel 12:1).

A Prayer Chain?

This is the chain of events will help to form the chain in the hand of the angel in Revelation, chapter 20, which "binds" the devil. Satan fears that chain. This is why he dreads God's church laying aside their pride and differences to actually come together on a global level to experience a global surge of prayer, Bible study, revival, and reformation in preparation for a global petitioning for the latter rain. Prayer is the mechanism that sets off the formation of that chain in the angel's hand. It all starts with God's people praying, globally. We may call it a global prayer chain.

God is waiting for the sign, the mechanism that sets the chain re-action into action. Already such global movements of prayer are taking formation in God's church. Ellen White saw such a reformation: "I have been deeply impressed by scenes that have recently passed before me in the night-season. There seemed to be a great movement—a work of revival—going forward in many places. Our people were moving into line, responding to God's call" (*The Review and Herald*, May 29, 1913).

If God's people around the globe take the call seriously, put away their sins, lay aside their pride, prejudices, and empty themselves by the grace of God, unbelievable things will happen because God has promised that it would be so. We will come to that moment of prayer, having experienced the early rain and, thus, being fitted to receive the latter rain. Let us humble ourselves, seeking God's face and power so that He may set into action that chain reaction. This will put that symbolic chain in the hand of the angel to bind the enemy and deliver His people once and for all. God is waiting for the signal.

> If my people, which are called by my name, shall humble themselves, and pray, and seek my face, and turn from their wicked ways; then will I hear from heaven, and will forgive their sin, and will heal their land. (2 Chronicles 7:14)

Group Discussion Questions

1. Review and discuss the chain of events.

2. What is it that sets off the chain reaction?

3. How can we as a church accomplish this "setting off"?

4. What impacted you most from this chapter?

Chapter 17
The War on Error

One of the most surprising factors of the parable of the ten virgins is the question of who comprises the five foolish virgins. Generally speaking, many Adventists believe that the five foolish virgins constitute those who are cold or lukewarm Seventh-day Adventists. While this is true, the five foolish virgins also include "hot" Adventists. They all at one time possessed "fire." When the disciples received the Holy Oil on the day of Pentecost, it lighted their lamps to go forth into a world of darkness. Ellen White said of this fire: "*The appearance of fire signified the fervent zeal* with which the apostles would labor and the power that would attend their work" (*The Acts of the Apostles*, 39)

> Through the grace of Christ, God's ministers are made messengers of light and blessing. As by earnest, persevering prayer they obtain the endowment of the Holy Spirit and go forth weighted with the burden of soul-saving, their hearts filled with zeal to extend the triumphs of the cross, they will see fruit of their labors. Resolutely refusing to display human wisdom or to exalt self, they will accomplish a work that will withstand the assaults of Satan. Many souls will be turned from darkness to light, and many churches will be established. Men will be converted, not to the human instrumentality, but to Christ. (*The Acts of the Apostles*, 278)

The five wise virgins, with their fire, will go forth to wage a war on error, the errors of Babylon. They will arise to shed the light of Calvary on the spiritual darkness brought about by the papacy. Their mission is to call God's people out of Babylon and into God's marvelous light. Speaking of this work done by the wise, Ellen White wrote:

> "Her sins have reached unto heaven, and God hath remembered her iniquities." [Revelation 18:5.] She has filled up the measure of her guilt, and destruction is about to fall upon her. But God still has a people in Babylon; and before the visitation of his judgments, these faithful ones must be called out, that they "partake not of her sins, and receive not of her plagues." Hence the

movement symbolized by the angel coming down from Heaven, lightening the earth with his glory, and crying mightily with a strong voice, announcing the sins of Babylon. In connection with his message the call is heard, "Come out of her, my people." As these warnings join the third angel's message, it swells to a loud cry. (*The Spirit of Prophecy*, 422)

However, the five foolish virgins also possess zeal. The foolish virgins, therefore, represent the spectrum of Adventists, from the cold, to the lukewarm, to the zealous. These zealous but foolish virgins are perhaps the most difficult to distinguish, and they are the most dangerous to themselves and others, in particular because of their influence, and *their appearance* as the cream of the crop or conservative Seventh-day Adventist. In the parable, the light of the five foolish is described as "going out" (Matthew 25:8 ESV).

In other words, their light did not go out at once. It was a process. The more one loses light, *or rejects it*, the harder it becomes to see. When they began to lose their spiritual sight, light began to appear as darkness to them. They began to fight as it were against the light, thinking they are fighting against error. Then just as the zeal of the five wise virgins led them to wage a war on error, the errors of Babylon, so the five foolish virgins, moved by an unholy zeal, began to wage a war on what they thought to be "error." Speaking of the foolish virgins, Ellen White said:

> Without the Spirit of God a knowledge of His word is of no avail. The theory of truth, unaccompanied by the Holy Spirit, cannot quicken the soul or sanctify the heart. One may be familiar with the commands and promises of the Bible; but unless the Spirit of God sets the truth home, the character will not be transformed. *Without the enlightenment of the Spirit, men will not be able to distinguish truth from error*, and they will fall under the masterful temptations of Satan. (*Christ's Object Lessons*, 408, emphasis added)

Today, on the left, many Adventists are waging a zealous war on what they think is error. In so doing, they are tearing down the foundations of the church. With fervent zeal, a war is being waged against the doctrine of the sanctuary, the biblical position on creation, homosexuality, the Spirit of Prophecy, the stance against magic and spiritualism, New Age philosophies, and more. Unfortunately, these are all signs of lights "going out."

On the other hand, the right, many so called conservatives, yet un-converted Seventh-day Adventists, *in their blindness* will become zealous in fighting against truth that they have come to think is error. Simply put, if Satan can quench the light in the lamp, he can then lead people to fight against truth under the deception that they are fighting *for truth*. Satan will work not only from the left, but also from the right. This is why we must be totally centered upon Christ.

> Satan is working with all his hellish power to quench that light which should burn brightly in the soul and shine forth in good works. *The words of God to Zechariah show from whence the holy golden oil comes*, and its bright light which the Lord kindles in the chambers of the soul gives light through good works to the world. Satan will work to quench the light God has for every soul, by casting his shadow across the pathway *to intercept every ray of heavenly light*. He knows that his time is short. … If they [the people of God] cherish hereditary and cultivated traits of charac-ter *that misrepresent Christ*, while professedly His disciples, they are represented by the man coming to the gospel feast without having on the wedding garment, and *by the foolish virgins* which had no oil in their vessels with their lamps. *We must cleave to that which God pronounces to be truth*, though the whole world may be arrayed against it. (*Seventh-day Adventist Bible Commentary*, vol. 4, 1179)

We do not want to be found under so strong a deception that we begin to call light darkness. But this is exactly what happens, even among conservative Adventists. Listen.

> There is to be in the [Seventh-day Adventist] churches a wonder-ful manifestation of the power of God, but it will not move upon those who have not humbled themselves before the Lord, and opened the door of the heart by confession and repentance. In the manifestation of that power which lightens the earth with the glory of God, they will see only something which in *their blind-ness* they think dangerous, something which will arouse their fears, and they will brace themselves to resist it. *Because the Lord does not work according to their ideas and expectations they will oppose the work*. "Why," they say, "should we not know the Spirit of God, when we have been in the work so many years?" (*The Review and Herald*, December 23, 1890, emphasis added)

Much like the Pharisees in the days of Christ, the foolish virgins will appear righteous, defenders of the truth, waging a war on so called "error," which is really the light of the third angel's message. This same misguided "war on error" was waged against the light given in 1888.

> In this time light from the throne of God has been long resisted as an objectionable thing. *It has been regarded as darkness* and spoke of as fanaticism, *as something dangerous, to be shunned.* Thus men have become guide-posts pointing in the wrong direction. They have followed the example *set by the Jewish people.* They have hugged their false theories and maxims to their hearts until they have become to them as precious fundamental doctrines. They have come to think that if they let them go, the foundations of their faith will be destroyed. If all those who *claim to believe present truth had opened their hearts to receive the message, and the spirit of truth,* which is the mercy and justice and love of God, *they would not have gathered about the darkness so dense that they could not discern light. They would not have called the operations of the Holy Spirit fanaticism and error.* (*The Ellen G. White 1888 Materials,* 915, 916, emphasis added)

The foolish virgins and the Pharisees both claimed light, but they did not bring it into their practical lives. In both groups it led to a loss of light. Ellen White wrote:

> Every specification of this parable should be carefully studied. We are represented either by the wise or by the foolish virgins. There are many who will not remain at the feet of Jesus, and learn of him. They have not a knowledge of his ways; they are not prepared for his coming. ... *They have heard and assented to the truth, but they have never brought it into their practical life.* (*The Review and Herald,* October 31, 1899, emphasis added)

The Pharisees, while claiming to possess the light, rejected it under a cloak of "zeal" for the truth. How? They discouraged the study of the Scriptures by those who were in their minds, *unauthorized* to do so. They felt that their knowledge was superior to the average Israelite. So when Christ came "having never learned" (John 7:15), they supposed that he had no business teaching.

The Pharisees scoffed at Christ; they criticized the simplicity of his language, which was so plain that the child, the aged, the common people heard him gladly, and were charmed by his words. The Sadducees also derided him because his discourses were so unlike anything delivered by their rulers and scribes. (*Christian Education*, 142)

The Spirit was upon Christ and taught Him personally. In the same manner God's Spirit will move upon His people in the last days to teach them personally.

God will work a work in our day that but few anticipate. He will raise up and exalt among us those who are taught rather by *the unction of His Spirit* than by the outward training of scientific institutions. These facilities are not to be despised or condemned; they are ordained of God, but they can furnish only the exterior qualifications. God will manifest that He is not dependent on learned, self-important mortals. ...

To souls that are earnestly seeking for light and that accept *with gladness* every ray of divine illumination from His holy Word, *to such alone* light will be given. It is through these souls that God *will reveal that light and power which will lighten the whole earth with His glory.* ... (*Last Day Events*, 204, 205, emphasis supplied)

Prideful Pharisees, who rejected the light of Christ's teachings by calling it darkness, fought against that light at every step. So the foolish virgins, blinded by zeal, will fight against the advancing light of the midnight cry given by those who they deem below themselves. They will do this by discouraging anything they feel goes beyond what they themselves have studied. In other words, they will seek to quench the spirit of discovery of advancing light in the Word of God. They will criticize and censure those who do not agree with their own previous findings.

Remember that it is because the Lord did not "work according to their ideas and expectations" that they end up opposing the light. In other words, the light did not come in a way or source from which they expected. They despised the light because it did not fit their ideas of how light should look, or how it should come. As Solomon put it: "The fear of the Lord is the beginning of knowledge: but fools despise wisdom and instruction" (Proverbs 1:7). It not so much that foolish did not have some knowledge, but rather that they refused to believe that anyone else could have knowledge above what they had.

The Pharisees despised the wisdom of Christ because they could not make sense of His spiritual words. So professed, conservative Adventists will block the light of the midnight cry because they think it impossible for God to have bypassed them to give it to the so-called simple or unlearned. While appearing to be wise, they actually scorn anything that they themselves have not discovered or seen.

> How long, ye simple ones, will ye love simplicity? and the scorners delight in their scorning, and fools hate knowledge? ... Wherefore is there a price in the hand of a fool to get wisdom, seeing he hath no heart to it? ... Speak not in the ears of a fool: for he will despise the wisdom of thy words. (Proverbs 1:22; 17:16; 23:9)

The danger for the Seventh-day Adventist who claims to have light is to be engaged in the habit of criticizing the light of his fellow brethren. He does this by making himself superior to others and tearing down the work of others.

> Those who are exacting, who are faultfinding, who think evil of others, are advancing the work of the enemy, tearing down that which God would have built up. All these discordant elements represent the powers of darkness, and show that Christ, the hope of glory, is not found within. (*Testimonies to Southern Africa*, 26)

The oil is what keeps the light burning. The oil represents the holy spirit. Proverbs 21:20 says, "There is treasure to be desired and oil in the dwelling of the wise; but a foolish man spendeth it up." The foolish "spend up" the oil in this sense. They believe that there is no more "treasure" or truth to be found than what has been revealed *to them*. They limit, therefore, or cut off, "spend up" the Holy Spirit by this attitude that there is nothing more for them to learn, especially from their brethren whom they consider inferior in knowledge. "Seest thou a man wise in his own conceit? there is more hope of a fool than of him" (Proverbs 26:12). Speaking of the increase of light from the scriptures, Sister White wrote:

> Then opened he their understanding, that they might understand the Scriptures." Before this opening of their understanding, the disciples had not understood the spiritual meaning of what Christ had taught them. And it is necessary now that the minds of God's people should be opened to understand the Scriptures. *To say that a passage means just this and nothing more, that you must not attach any broader meaning to the words of Christ than we have in the past, is saying that which is not actuated by the Spirit of God.* The more we *walk in the light of the truth*, the more we shall

become like Christ in spirit in character and in the manner of our work, and *the brighter will the truth become to us*. As we behold it *in the increasing light of revelation*, it will become more precious than we first estimated it from a casual hearing or examination. The truth, as it is in Jesus, is capable of constant expansion, of new development, and like its divine Author it will become more precious and beautiful; it will constantly reveal deeper significance, and lead the soul to aspire for more perfect conformity to its exalted standard. *Such understanding of the truth will elevate the mind and transform the character to its divine perfection.* (*The Review and Herald*, October 21, 1890, emphasis added)

The foolish virgins despised the treasure of truth simply because of pride. "Why," they say, "should we not know the Spirit of God, when we have been in the work so many years?" (*Last Day Events*, 209).

Thus will be fulfilled the words of Daniel, "Many shall be purified, and made white, and tried; but the wicked shall do wickedly: and none of the wicked shall understand; but the wise shall understand" (Daniel 12:10). Incidentally, this was the very spirit of those who fought what they thought to be a ar on error against A. T. Jones and E. J. Waggoner during the 1888 meetings in which both men presented light that had been new to the hearers. Of this class, we read:

The enemy has been at work seeking to control the thoughts, the affections, and the spiritual eyesight of many who claim to be led by the *Spirit of truth*, Many cherish unkind thoughts, envyings, evil surmisings, pride, and a fierce spirit that leads them to do works corresponding to the works of the wicked one. They have a love of authority, a desire for preeminence, for a high reputation, a disposition to censure and revile others. And the garment of hypocrisy is thrown over *this spirit* by calling *it zeal for the truth*. ... Let no one among you glory any longer against the truth by pretending that this spirit is a necessary consequence of faithfulness in righting wrongs and standing in defense of the truth. Such wisdom has many admirers, but it is very deceptive and harmful. It does not come from above, but is the fruit of a heart that needs regeneration. Its originator is Satan himself. Do not give yourselves, *as accusers of others*, credit for discernment; for you clothe the attributes of Satan with the garments of righteousness. I call upon you, my brethren, to purify the soul temple from all these things that defile. They are roots of bitterness. (*Manuscript Releases*, vol. 15, 180, emphasis added)

Some who think that they preach the gospel are preaching other men's ideas. Through some means they have come to the decision that it is no part of a minister's calling or duty to think diligently and prayerfully. He accepts what other men have taught without asserting his individuality. *This doctrine, taught by the church of Rome,* is entire dependence upon the leaders. The individual's conscience is not his own. Judgment must be controlled by other men's ideas. His intelligence is to go no farther than that of those who are leaders.

Now Satan has his hand in all this work to narrow down the work of God. Ministers of Jesus Christ are to be constantly receiving light from the Source of all light. They are not to be simply receivers of other men's thoughts, they themselves not plowing deep into the mines of truth. If a minister is not a worker himself, digging for the truth as for hidden treasure to find the precious jewels of truth, he is forfeiting his God-given privileges. He is not to put any human mind, any human intelligence, between his soul and God. There is to come no authority from human minds that will in the least degree interpose between him and God's authority to lead, to guide, and to dictate. The ministers of Christ should gather up every ray of light, every jot of strength and illumination from other minds whom God has blessed, but that is not enough. They must go to the Fountainhead for themselves. God has given men reasoning minds and He will not hold them guiltless if they trust in man or make flesh their arm. He wants you individually to come to Him, to draw from Him, to use the ability God gives to understand the living oracles. *If one man can see light in examining the Scriptures, so may every true Christian have the right to read, to examine, to search the Scriptures with unabated interest, and gather light therefrom.* (*The Ellen G. White 1888 Materials,* 834, 835, emphasis added)

The oil represents the spirit. But the zealous yet foolish virgins come to possess or be possessed by another spirit. In fact, the five foolish virgins, in warring against the search for new light end up possessing the very spirit of Babylon.

Shall there be with the people of God the cropping out of *the very same spirit* which they have condemned in the denominations, because there was a difference of understanding on some points—not vital questions? Shall the *same spirit* in any form be cherished among Seventh-day Adventists—the cooling of friendship, the withdrawal of confidence, the misrepresentation of motives, the endeavor to thwart and turn into ridicule those who honestly differ with them in their views? ...

Godliness, which the gospel enjoins, never bears briars and thorns, never—because all do not see exactly alike—breaks the closest links of association, dividing those who have been one in faith, one in heart, in their relationship. *But a difference in the application of some few scriptural passages makes men forget their religious principles.*_Elements become banded together, exciting one another through the human passions to withstand in a harsh, denunciatory manner everything that does not meet their ideas. *This is not Christian, but is of another spirit.* (*Manuscript Releases*, 331, 332, emphasis added)

Of this spirit, which was present at the 1888 meetings, Ellen White wrote that the angel of the Lord said to her:

There was a spirit coming in taking possession of the churches, that if permitted would separate them from God ...

I have been shown that the people of God are not fully enlightened in regard to the many devices of the relentless foe whom they will have to encounter. ... There is a great, grand charge to be made by a united front against the enemy and Satan has great victories because there is a difference in views in our ranks upon some points of Scripture not (of) a vital character. *Men who claim to believe the truth*, I have been shown, will develop their true standing before God. My guide said, "Follow me." I was then taken to the different houses where our people made their homes. *I heard the conversation, the remarks, made in reference to myself*; the testimonies borne at that meeting were commented upon. W.C.W. was talked of and presented in a most ridiculous light. I could define the speakers by their voices. A. T. Jones was commented upon in like manner, so was E. J. Waggoner, Said my guide, "Where is the earnest prayer, the seeking of God with humble heart for light?" I was listening in the different rooms to the sarcastic remarks, unchristian comments, the excitable, exaggerated statements made all because that there was a difference in the views of the law in Galatians. O consistency, hast thou departed from the midst of Seventh-day Adventists? After listening some time to the free, unchristlike words, then my work was appointed me.

I was told this spirit had been gathering strength for years and the leavening influence was at work and spiritual life was going out of the churches. (*The Ellen G. White 1888 Materials*, 296, 297, emphasis added)

The Pharisaic spirit is considered to be "the greatest evil" that could enter the church.

As a people we are certainly in great danger, if we are not constantly guarded, of considering our ideas, because long cherished, to be Bible doctrines and on every point infallible, and measuring everyone by the rule of our interpretation of Bible truth. This is our danger, and *this would be the greatest evil that could ever come to us as a people.* If one should hold ideas differing in some respects from that which we have heretofore entertained—not on vital points of truth—there should not be a firm, rigid attitude assumed that all is right in every particular, all is Bible truth without a flaw, that every point we have held is without mistake or cannot be improved. This I know to be dangerous business and it proceeds from that wisdom that is from beneath. (*The Ellen G. White 1888 Materials*, 830, emphasis added)

The Wise Way to Approach Differences

To be sure, not everything that presents itself as light should be regarded as light from God. We must test the spirits. However, there is a wise way to do so as well as a foolish way. Each of us belongs to one of these groups or the other, and the methods that we choose reveals to which group of the virgins we belong.

If a brother differ with you on some points of truth, do not stoop to ridicule, do not place him in a false light, or misconstrue his words, making sport of them; do not misinterpret his words and wrest them of their true meaning. This is not conscientious argument. Do not present him before others as a heretic, when you have not with him investigated his positions, taking the Scriptures text by text in the spirit of Christ to show him what is truth. You do not yourself really know the evidence he has for his faith, and you cannot really clearly define your own position. Take your Bible, and in a kindly spirit weigh every argument that he presents and show him by the Scriptures if he is in error. *When you do this without unkind feelings, you will do only that which is your duty and the duty of every minister of Jesus Christ.* (*Counsels to Writers and Editors*, 50, 51, emphasis supplied)

Suppose a brother held a view that differed from yours, and he should come to you, proposing that you sit down with him and make an investigation of that point in the Scriptures; should you rise up, filled with prejudice, and condemn his ideas, while refusing to give him a candid hearing?

The only right way would be to sit down as Christians and investigate the position presented, in the light of God's word, which will reveal truth and unmask error. To ridicule his ideas would not weaken his position in the least if it were false, or strengthen your position if it were true. If the pillars of our faith will not stand the test of investigation, it is time that we knew it. *There must be no spirit of pharisaism* cherished among us. When Christ came to His own, His own received Him not; and it is a matter of solemn interest to us that we should not pursue a similar course *in refusing light from heaven.* (*Counsels to Writers and Editors*, 44, 45, emphasis supplied)

Speaking of the way Waggoner was treated by fellow Adventists zealous for "truth," Ellen White wrote:

Of one thing I am certain, as Christians you have no right to entertain feelings of enmity, unkindness, and prejudice toward Dr. Waggoner, who has presented his views in a plain, straightforward manner, as a Christian should. *If he is in error, you should, in a calm, rational, Christlike manner, seek to show him from the Word of God where he is out of harmony with its teachings. If you cannot do this you have no right* as Christians to pick flaws, to criticize, to work in the dark, to prejudice minds with your objections. *This is Satan's way of working.*

Some interpretations of Scripture given by Dr. Waggoner I do not regard as correct. But I believe him to be perfectly honest in his views, and I would respect his feelings and treat him as a Christian gentleman. I have no reason to think that he is not as much esteemed of God as are any of my brethren, and I shall regard him as a Christian brother, so long as there is no evidence that he is unworthy. *The fact that he honestly holds some views of Scripture differing from yours or mine is no reason why we should treat him as an offender,* or as a dangerous man, and make him the subject of unjust criticism. *We should not raise a voice of censure* against him or his teachings unless we can present *weighty reasons* for so doing and show him that he is in error. No one should feel at liberty to give loose rein to the combative spirit. (*The Ellen G. White 1888 Materials,* 163, 164, emphasis added)

The five foolish virgins thought that they were standing in defense of the truth when, like the Pharisees, their pride and self exaltation disqualified them from receiving any further light. Conservative Adventists who claim to believe present truth will manifest the spirit of Rome in dealing with those who disagree with them. In the end they were inadvertently blinded by a spirit of darkness.

As the storm approaches, a large class who have professed faith in the third angel's message, but have not been sanctified through obedience to the truth, abandon their position, and join the ranks of the opposition. By uniting with the world and *partaking of its spirit, they have come* to view matters in nearly the same light; and when the test is brought, they are prepared to choose the easy, popular side. *Men of talent and pleasing address, who once rejoiced in the truth,* employ their powers to deceive and mislead souls. *They become the most bitter enemies of their former brethren.* (*The Great Controversy,* 608, emphasis supplied)

Group Discussion Questions

1. Why were the Pharisees warring against Jesus?

2. How is that same spirit present in the church today?

3. Why is it dangerous to believe that God can only work through the best and most educated?

4. How should we test light brought to us?

5. How should we treat our brethren who may differ from on us certain points that do not contradict the fundamentals of our faith?

6. Why should we encourage the free study of the Word of God?

7. What impacted you most about this chapter?

Chapter 18
When He Dies, It Shall Be Sent

W hat creates the conditions to bring about these powerful end-time tidings out of the symbolic east and the north? The answer may lie in an obscure but godly man of the Old Testament. In the time just before the flood, there lived a man who was a type of walking prophecy. His name was Methuselah, Noah's grandfather.

His name is found in the genealogy of Genesis chapter 5. There are two schools of thought as to the meaning of the name Methuselah. Some believe the name means, "man of the spear," *meth* coming from the Hebrew word *math*, meaning "man," and *shâlach*, is "a primitive root; [meaning] to send away, for, or out (in a great variety of applications): -X any wise, appoint, *bring* (on the way), ... send (away, forth, out), set, shoot (forth, out), sow, spread, stretch forth (out)." [4]

However, *The Exhaustive Dictionary of Bible Names* gives the definition of Methuselah as "when he is dead it shall be sent," meaning the flood. [5] The same name appears in the New Testament genealogy of Christ in its Greek form *Mathusala* (see Luke 3:37). According to the Thayer's New Testament lexicon [6], the Greek version of *Mathusala* means "when he dies, there shall be an emission." This is because *methu* comes from the Hebrew *muth* meaning "death." Hence, the name has been translated to mean: "when he dies, it will be sent," and by others as "his death will bring," signifying that upon his death *the flood would come.* (See Louis F. Were's *The Certainty of the Third Angel's Message*, 181.)

"Enoch thus named his son using two Hebrew roots: *muth*, which means "his death," and *shelac*, which is a verb form that means "bring," or "sent forth." So the name Methuselah means, "his death shall bring." The flood of Noah did not come as a surprise; it had been predicted for four generations." [7]

4   *Strong's Concordance*, emphasis added.

5   Judson Cornwall and Stelman Smith, *The Exhaustive Dictionary of Bible Names* (Alachua, FL: Bridge-Logos, 1988), 133.

6   Joseph Henry Thayer, D.D. , *A Greek-English Lexicon of the New Testament* (New York: American Book Company, 1886, 1889), accessed from e-Sword software, version 10.1.0.

7   Chuck Missler, *Learn the Bible in 24 Hours* (Nashville, TN: Thomas Nelson, Inc., 2002), 24.

The prophetic significance of the name is recognized by well known scholars. Bible commentator John Gill wrote, "Enoch being a prophet gave him this [Methuselah] name under a spirit of prophecy, foretelling by it when the flood should be; for his name, according to Bochart (s), signifies, 'when he dies there shall be an emission,' or sending forth of waters upon the earth, to destroy it." [8]

Jamieson, Fausset, Brown's commentary says, "Enoch ... begat Methuselah — This name signifies, 'He dieth, and the sending forth,' so that Enoch gave it as prophetical of the flood. It is computed that Methuselah died in the year of that catastrophe." [9] Also, Adam Clarke commentary says this in commenting on Genesis 5:32: "Methuselah lived till the very year in which the flood came, of which his name is supposed to have been prophetical ותמ methu, "he dieth," and חלש shalach, "he sendeth out;" as if God had designed to teach men that as soon as Methuselah died the flood should be sent forth to drown an ungodly world. If this were then so understood, even the name of this patriarch contained in it a gracious warning." [10]

Methuselah died in the very year that the flood was sent. He was 369 when Noah was born, and died at 969 years old, when Noah was 600. It was the 600th year of Noah's life when the flood came (Genesis 5:21–29; 7:11).

The flood came upon the heels of Methuselah's death. That this godly saint Methuselah also serves as type of Christ is seen in the fact that just as in the very year that he died, the flood came, or was sent. In the very year that Christ died, the Holy Spirit flooded the earth at Pentecost as recorded in the book of Acts, chapter 2. Christ told His disciples that if He did not go away, the Spirit would not come (John 16:7). On the day of Pentecost, this very verse was fulfilled. "I will pour water upon him that is thirsty, and floods upon the dry ground: I will pour My Spirit upon thy seed, and My blessing upon thine offspring" (Isaiah 44:3).

This outpouring represents the early rain, which was poured upon the New Testament church at the beginning of its existence. So at the end of time, there will be an outpouring of the latter rain, which brings the work of the church to its fruition and prepares it for the heavenly harvester, Jesus Christ (see Revelation 14:14–16). Then, just as it was Christ's

---

8   John Gill, *Complete Body of Practical and Doctrinal Divinity* (Philadelphia: Delaplaine and Hellings, 1810), accessed from e-Sword software, version 10.1.0.

9   *Commentary Critical and Explanatory on the Whole Bible*, accessed from e-Sword software, version 10.1.0.

10 Adam Clarke, *Commentary and Critical Notes* (New York: J. Emory and B. Waugh for the Methodist Episcopal Church, 1829), accessed from e-Sword software, version 10.1.0.

death that brought the early rain, we shall soon see that it is an understanding and practical application of Christ's death. Christ lifted up, as it relates to the three angels' messages, will bring about the latter rain, the "nor'easter," the glad tidings of Daniel 11:44.

The book of Zechariah records the fact that a view of Christ pierced is closely connected with the repentance needed for the outpouring of his Spirit.

> I will pour upon the house of David, and upon the inhabitants of Jerusalem, the spirit of grace and of supplications: and they shall look upon me whom they have pierced, and they shall mourn for him, as one mourneth for his only son, and shall be in bitterness for him, as one that is in bitterness for his firstborn. (Zechariah 2:10)

When the cross of Christ and His sacrifice are seen in the true import, the vision of the two olive trees with the Lamp tree at its center is clearly understood and lived out. We will "weep" between the porch and the altar (Joel 2); weep because of our transgressions against Him; weep because of our distrust, our indifference, our sleepiness. Yes, the measure of His sacrifice fully comprehended and realized by us as a people will bring the great outpouring depicted in Zechariah 2:10.

> The soul who appreciates the precious gift of salvation will ever behold Christ dying upon the cross, and the language of that soul will be the language of unselfish sorrow that he has ever committed sin to so wound the Son of God. I shall always grieve that I have sinned, and have cost the Man of Calvary so great anguish. I look upon him whom I have pierced, and I mourn that I have transgressed the law of God. When we have a proper appreciation of the sacrifice that has been made in our behalf, we shall not plead for the privilege of continuing in transgression. We shall put away sin, and our hard hearts will melt under the amazing love of Christ for our souls. (*The Signs of the Times*, October 28, 1889)

This putting away of sin is the condition for receiving the latter rain, something that can only be done by looking upon Him whom we have pierced. In this way, His death will indeed bring the outpouring. Then "the earth shall be filled with the knowledge of the glory of the Lord, as the waters cover the sea" (Habakkuk 2:14).

The "knowledge of the glory" of the Lord that will cover the earth like a flood is the same "glory" we are called to give to God in the first angel's message. It is the same "glory" with which the angel of Revelation, chapter 18, will descend to lighten the earth.

> The power of the proclamation of the first and second messages is to be concentrated in the third. In the Revelation, John says of the angel that unites with the third angel: "I saw another angel come down from heaven, having great power, and the earth was lightened with his glory. And he cried mightily with a strong voice. (*Testimonies for the Church*, vol. 6, 60)

> I saw another mighty angel commissioned to descend to the earth, to unite his voice with the third angel, and give power and force to his message. (*The Faith I Live By*, 335)

This angel will descend with light, renewed light, for the virgins trim their lamps. We are told to expect new light. Yet, we are also told that this new light is really old light that has been overlooked. The new light we are told is "precious old light to shine forth from the Word of truth."

> The question has been asked me, "Do you think that the Lord has any more light for us as a people?" I answer that He has light that is new to us, and yet it is precious old light that is to shine forth from the Word of truth. We have only the glimmerings of the rays of the light that is yet to come to us. We are not making the most of the light which the Lord has already given us, and thus we fail to receive the increased light; we do not walk in light already shed upon us. (*Selected Messages*, Book 1, 401, 402)

The message that his angel descends to give is a message focused on "power" and "glory." It is a message pointing to the Lamp tree between the two anointed cherubs. Notice the "power" of this message.

> For I am not ashamed of the gospel of Christ: for it is the power of God unto salvation to every one that believeth; to the Jew first, and also to the Greek. (Romans 1:16)

The gospel of Christ is the "power" of God. But what exactly is the gospel? Paul said:

For Christ sent me not to baptize, but to preach the gospel: not with wisdom of words, lest the cross of Christ should be made of none effect. For the preaching of the cross is to them that perish foolishness; but unto us which are saved it is the power of God. (1 Corinthians 1:17, 18)

The preaching of the gospel is used interchangeably with the preaching of the cross. Thus, the cross, Christ, and Him crucified is the power of God. It is the preaching of the cross when added to the three angels' messages that will add power, a convincing power and an undeniable power, to the certainty and truthfulness of our message. His death gives power to our message. The five wise virgins advanced with power to their message, having trimmed their light to focus specifically on Christ and Him crucified, both theoretically, and practically in connection with the three angels' messages.

Concerning the glory, Paul wrote, "God forbid that I should glory, save in the cross of our Lord Jesus Christ, by whom the world is crucified unto me, and I unto the world" (Galatians 6:14). The greatest glory of all is the cross of Christ. God's glory is synonymous with His character, and the greatest manifestation of His character is found at the cross. His death not only provides power to the three angels' messages, it also gives glory. This is the final message that is to go to the world.

> The last rays of merciful light, the last message of mercy to be given to the world, is a revelation of His character of love. The children of God are to manifest His glory. In their own life and character they are to reveal what the grace of God has done for them. (*Christ's Object Lessons*, 415)

The message of this fourth angel was foreign to the foolish virgins, who had felt that they were "rich" in the truths of God's Word. They had not made Christ the center but rather the book ends of the message and their lifestyle. Our doctrines must be preached centered in the cross of Christ, and then it will go forth in blazing power, drawing thousands upon thousands into the truth at an astonishingly rapid rate. Concerning this very problem, Ellen White wrote:

> Of all professing Christians, Seventh-day Adventists should be foremost in uplifting Christ before the world. The proclamation of the third angel's message calls for the presentation of the Sabbath truth. This truth, with others included in the message, is to be proclaimed; but the great center of attraction, Christ Jesus,

must not be left out. It is at the cross of Christ that mercy and truth meet together, and righteousness and peace kiss each other. The sinner must be led to look to Calvary; with the simple faith of a little child he must trust in the merits of the Saviour, accepting His righteousness, believing in His mercy. (*Gospel Workers*, 156, 157)

This message was to bring more prominently before the world the uplifted Saviour, the sacrifice for the sins of the whole world. … Centuries, ages, can never diminish the efficacy of this atoning sacrifice. The message of the gospel of His grace was to be given to the church in clear and distinct lines, that the world should no longer say that Seventh-day Adventists talk the law, the law, but do not teach or believe Christ. (*Evangelism*, 190, 191)

Now is the time for God's people to preach the new light of the old rugged cross. Through His death, power and glory is added to the three angels' messages. Our message will then go forth as fire in the stubble because it will be centered and coupled with His death on the cross.

The angel of Revelation 18:1–4 descends with "great power"—the power of God. This "power of God" (the cross), added to the three angels' messages, will create the most powerful nor'easter the world will ever witness. The nor'easter will be loosed, and by focusing upon His death on the cross, and the victory attained through it, the Spirit will be sent; the flood will come, God's power shall be sent.

The message will revolve around the cross of Calvary with the sole purpose of pointing people to the great sacrifice. The flood of His light will rain upon the earth. God's people, armed with the glory of the cross, which is the "power of God," will go forth successfully calling His people out of Babylon. We will be given a large measure of the Spirit for a specific purpose.

The Spirit is given as a regenerating agency, to make effectual the salvation wrought by the death of our Redeemer. The Spirit is constantly seeking to draw the attention of men to the great offering that was made on the cross of Calvary, to unfold to the world the love of God, and to open to the convicted soul the precious things of the Scriptures. (*The Acts of the Apostles*, 52, emphasis added)

"Presenting the cross of Calvary, we are to cry, 'Behold the Lamb of God, which taketh away the sin of the world.' When we shall cease to trust in man, and shall make God our efficiency, we shall see the earth filled with the glory of the Lord as the waters cover the sea" (*The Review and Herald*, October 16, 1900). So by obtaining the power of the cross, we will see the promise of the Scripture fulfilled beyond our imagination: "I, if I be lifted up from the earth, will draw all men unto me" (John 12:32).

One hundred twenty years after Noah, a "preacher of righteousness" (2 Peter 2:5) and heir of "righteousness which is by faith" (Hebrews 11:7), began to preach, the flood came. It has been more than 120 years since the tidings of righteousness by faith began to brew from the northeast back in 1888.

My appeal is that we will look upon Him whom we have pierced and put away our indifferences, our sleepiness, and our sins. In so doing, we may then take the news of God's character and law as revealed in the cross, combining it with the three angels' messages, to the entire world. Let us trim our lamps, and focus on the very center of the third angel's message, Christ lifted up. It is time for the final nor'easter, time for the flood.

Group Discussion Questions

1. How is the cross the center of the latter rain?

2. Why is the cross so central to the latter rain?

3. What about the cross is to lighten the whole world with glory?

4. What impacted you most from this chapter?

Chapter 19
The Chief Cornerstone and the
Final Work of Seventh-day Adventists

The work of the Seventh-day Adventist church parallels the history of ancient Israel. As Israel was called out of Babylon to begin to rebuild the temple, so Seventh-day Adventists have been called out of false systems to rebuild the true temple, the spiritual church upon earth. This church is comprised of God's people. "Ye also, as lively stones, are built up a spiritual house, an holy priesthood, to offer up spiritual sacrifices, acceptable to God by Jesus Christ" (1 Peter 2:5).

This temple is also built upon the Word of God, the doctrines that make up the church. "Therefore whosoever heareth these sayings of mine, and doeth them, I will liken him unto a wise man, which built his house upon a rock: And the rain descended, and the floods came, and the winds blew, and beat upon that house; and it fell not: for it was founded upon a rock" (Matthew 7:24, 25).

Since 1844, thousands have been making the exodus out of Babylon, and into spiritual Israel to help in rebuilding the true teachings of the Word of God, known to us as the three angels' messages. When the initial decree went forth allowing ancient Israel to return from Babylon to Jerusalem, relatively few were willing to leave the comforts of Babylon to set out and do the work of the Lord. Even now, there are many who have become comfortable with the ways of the world, slowing down the rebuilding process of the three angels' messages.

Another lesson that is crucial for us to understand parallels the building of the first temple, Solomon's Temple. Ellen White explained it this way:

> In quoting the prophecy of the rejected stone, Christ referred to an actual occurrence in the history of Israel. The incident was connected with the building of the first temple. While it had a special application at the time of Christ's first advent, and should have appealed with special force to the Jews, it has also a lesson for us. When the temple of Solomon was erected, the immense stones for the walls and the foundation were entirely prepared at the quarry; after they were brought to the place of building, not an instrument was to be used upon them; the workmen had only to place them in position. For use in the foundation, one

stone of unusual size and peculiar shape had been brought; but the workmen could find no place for it, and would not accept it. It was an annoyance to them as it lay unused in their way. Long it remained a rejected stone. But when the builders came to the laying of the corner, they searched for a long time to find a stone of sufficient size and strength, and of the proper shape, to take that particular place, and bear the great weight which would rest upon it. Should they make an unwise choice for this important place, the safety of the entire building would be endangered. They must find a stone capable of resisting the influence of the sun, of frost, and of tempest. Several stones had at different times been chosen, but under the pressure of immense weights they had crumbled to pieces. Others could not bear the test of the sudden atmospheric changes. But at last attention was called to the stone so long rejected. It had been exposed to the air, to sun and storm, without revealing the slightest crack. The builders examined this stone. It had borne every test but one. If it could bear the test of severe pressure, they decided to accept it for the cornerstone. The trial was made. The stone was accepted, brought to its assigned position, and found to be an exact fit. (*The Desire of Ages*, 597, 598)

Since 1844, the Seventh-day Adventist church has built a magnificent structure of truth based upon the Word of God. Yet, there seems to have been one Stone excluded from the structure. It's nearby, but not the center. It has seemed to some to be in the way, a minor Stone compared to the grand truths of the Sabbath, state of the dead, and the 2,300-day prophecy. Forty-four years later, in 1888, some began take more notice of this Stone—Christ our righteousness. Christ and Him crucified was brought to the attention of the church. Still, the Stone seemed out of place, awkward, and in fact overlooked as something vital. After all, what church doesn't believe Christ died and was resurrected? This was precious truth but certainly not *present truth.*

Our center focus was not the cross; it was the law of God—the distinct message of Seventh-day Adventism. The Stone was set aside as we continued to build. So here we are more than 120 years later, still wondering why the glory of the Lord has not filled the temple as it did in the days of Solomon. The structure of Seventh-day Adventism is almost complete, but one Stone remains out of place. We are one Stone away from a complete message to give this world—Christ and Him crucified.

Hanging upon the cross Christ was the gospel. Now we have a message, "Behold the Lamb of God, which taketh away the sins of the world." Will not our church members keep their eyes fixed on a crucified and risen Saviour, in whom their hopes of eternal life are centered? *This is our message, our argument, our doctrine, our warning to the impenitent, our encouragement for the sorrowing, the hope for every believer.* If we can awaken an interest in men's minds that will cause them to fix their eyes on Christ, *we may step aside, and ask them only to continue to fix their eyes upon the Lamb of God.* They thus receive their lesson. Whosoever will come after Me, let him deny himself, and take up his cross, and follow Me. He whose eyes are fixed on Jesus will leave all. He will die to selfishness. He will believe in all the Word of God, which is so gloriously and wonderfully exalted in Christ. (*Manuscript Releases*, vol. 21, 37, emphasis added)

He must become the center of the third angels' message. The remainder of this book will reveal Christ and Him crucified as the cornerstone of our message. When the final stone is put in place, the glory of the Lord will fill the temple.

Group Discussion Questions

1. Discuss what impacted you most from this chapter.

2. How do we make Christ the book ends and not the center?

3. What will focusing on Christ sacrifice do for us as a church?

4. What is the significance of Christ death in relation to the outpouring of God's Spirit?

Chapter 20
The Cross-centered Prophecies of Daniel

The angel of Revelation 18:1 will descend with a message that is to first enlighten and empower Seventh-day Adventists. It will also add power to the preaching of the last-day message. That special new light is the old rugged cross—Christ, the chief Cornerstone. Christ, lifted up on the cross, is to be made the primary point and focus of the three angels' messages. No sincere Christian can long resist the drawing of the cross. In this chapter, we will see the prophecies of Daniel in the new light of the old rugged cross.

The Cross and Daniel 2

The prophecy of Daniel 2 speaks of King Nebuchadnezzar's dream of a great statue with a head of gold, chest and arms of silver, belly and thighs of brass, legs of iron, toes of iron and clay. Each of these sections represents kingdoms at war with one another: respectively, Babylon, Medo-Persia, Greece, Rome, and divided Rome. The main point of Daniel 2 in our preaching has been to point out how God knows the future. While this is an important point of understanding, it does not focus upon the main purpose of the prophecy. That is no individual, nor kingdom can stand without Christ and will only deteriorate in value as the image itself deteriorated in value.

Notice verse 40, speaking of Rome, the iron kingdom: "The fourth kingdom shall be strong as iron: forasmuch as iron breaketh in pieces and subdueth all things: and as iron that breaketh all these, shall it break in pieces and bruise." Rome is said to do two things: "break" and "bruise." Daniel 11:22 parallels this account, referring to Rome having "broken" "the prince of the covenant," Jesus Christ: "With the arms of a flood shall they be overflown from before him, and shall be broken; yea, also the prince of the covenant."

Rome was the world power under which Christ lived upon earth. Jesus came to set up a kingdom "not of this world" (John 18:36). In response, Rome broke and bruised Christ. Christ, at the last supper, said, "Take, eat: this is my body, which is broken for you: this do in remembrance of me" (1 Corinthians 11:24). Isaiah 53:5 states, "But he was wounded for our transgressions, he was bruised for our iniquities: the chastisement of our peace was upon him; and with his stripes we are healed."

Rome, in connection with the leaders of Israel, rejected the chief Cornerstone. They rejected the sacrifice of Christ on their behalf. All nations since then have been warring against Christ's right to rule in their hearts, a right gained at the cross.

Christ said of the Jews, whom He knew would ultimately reject Him: "Did ye never read in the scriptures, The stone which the builders rejected, the same is become the head of the corner: this is the Lord's doing, and it is marvelous in our eyes? Therefore say I unto you, The kingdom of God shall be taken from you, and given to a nation bringing forth the fruits thereof. And whosoever shall fall on this stone shall be broken: but on whomsoever it shall fall, it will grind him to powder" (Matthew 21:42–44). It's no wonder then that the stone cut out without hands in Nebuchadnezzar's dream, grinds the image into powder—they had rejected the sacrifice of Christ.

> On "whomsoever it shall fall, it will grind him to powder." The people who rejected Christ were soon to see their city and their nation destroyed. ... So it will be in the great final day, when judgment shall fall upon the rejecters of God's grace. Christ, their rock of offense, will then appear to them as an avenging mountain. The glory of His countenance, which to the righteous is life, will be to the wicked a consuming fire. Because of love rejected, grace despised, the sinner will be destroyed. (*The Desire of Ages*, 600)

In like manner, any man who rejects the sacrifice of Christ will be ground into powder at the second coming of Christ. The wise thing to do is to accept His sacrifice.

The Cross and Daniel 7

The prophecy found in Daniel 7 is an amplification of Daniel 2. It again points out that this fourth kingdom, "brake in pieces" (Daniel 7:7). It leads us to the blasphemous action spoken of in Daniel 7:25: "He shall speak great words against the most High, and shall wear out the saints of the most High, and think to change times and laws." The focus is on the changing of "laws." Isaiah told us that this is the very reason the earth will be destroyed.

> Behold, the Lord maketh the earth empty, and maketh it waste, and turneth it upside down, and scattereth abroad the inhabitants thereof. The land shall be utterly emptied, and utterly spoiled: for the Lord hath spoken this word. The earth mourneth

and fadeth away, the world languisheth and fadeth away, the haughty people of the earth do languish. The earth also is defiled under the inhabitants thereof; because they have transgressed the laws, changed the ordinance, broken the everlasting covenant. Therefore hath the curse devoured the earth, and they that dwell therein are desolate: therefore the inhabitants of the earth are burned, and few men left. (Isaiah 24:1, 3–6)

This covenant is synonymous with the law of God (see Hebrews 8:8–10), but the covenant was sealed by the sacrifice of Christ. "He took the cup, and gave thanks, and gave it to them, saying, Drink ye all of it; For this is my blood of the new testament, which is shed for many for the remission of sins" (Matthew 26:27, 28). Christ died to seal the covenant. To attack the covenant is to attack the cross.

Daniel 7 has been historically used to focus upon antichrist's attack against the law of God. Under the loud cry, this prophecy must be used to reveal antichrist's attack upon the cross. To accept a change of the covenant is to reject the cross of Christ. The prophecy of Daniel 7 appeals to us to be wise and keep His commandments. "Thou through thy commandments hast made me wiser than mine enemies: for they are ever with me" (Psalm 119:98).

The Cross and Daniel 8:14

Daniel 8:14 has been the key contribution of Seventh-day Adventism to the Christian world: "He said unto me, Unto two thousand and three hundred days; then shall the sanctuary be cleansed." This prophecy has been historically used to show that the judgment began in 1844. But have we missed the focus? What is the Christian's hope in this trying time? What was the only hope of the children of Israel on the typical Day of Atonement? How was the sanctuary to be cleansed?

"He shall sprinkle of the blood upon it with his finger seven times, and cleanse it, and hallow it from the uncleanness of the children of Israel" (Leviticus 16:19). The blood of the sacrificed animal was the only hope on the Day of Atonement. So in the antitypical day of atonement, the 2,300-day prophecy is to point a people not only to the broken law of God but also to the shed blood of Christ, which cleanses us from all unrighteousness.

The fact is that the 2,300-day prophecy is about the restoration of truth going forth into the world. While the sanctuary in heaven is being in cleansed, the earthly temple of truth is being rebuilt. The Cornerstone of that truth, Christ and Him crucified, must be taken to the world. The world does not understand the purpose of the cross. Christ died for the remission of sins (see Matthew 26:28). That is, the purpose of the cross of Christ is to cleanse us from lawlessness. If it does not do this, it is a counterfeit covenant. The true purpose of the cross must be made plain through the 2,300-day prophecy.

The Cross and Daniel 9

The prophecy of Daniel 9 clearly speaks of Christ coming to "confirm the covenant" (see Daniel 9:27). Under the loud cry, we stress the importance that the covenant was confirmed by the cross or blood of Jesus (see Matthew 26:28). Again, to accept a change, any change in the covenant is to reject the cross and blood of Christ. Paul wrote, "Brethren, I speak after the manner of men; Though it be but a man's covenant, yet if it be confirmed, no man disannulleth, or addeth thereto" (Galatians 3:15).

A careful reading of Daniel 9 also reveals that Daniel becomes a type of Christ by the prayer he offered up on behalf of his people. Though there is no *record* of Daniel sinning, he assumed the sins of Israel as his own. In his petition he identified himself fully with those who had fallen short of the divine purpose, confessing their sins as his own.

I set my face unto the Lord God," the prophet declared, "to seek by prayer and supplications, with fasting, and sackcloth, and ashes: and I prayed unto the Lord my God, and made my confession." … Though Daniel had long been in the service of God, and had been spoken of by heaven as "greatly beloved," yet he now appeared before God as a sinner, urging the great need of the people he loved. (*Prophets and Kings*, 555)

Compare this with Christ.

Christ came not confessing his own sins; but guilt was imputed to him as the sinner's substitute. He came not to repent on his own account; but in behalf of the sinner. As man had transgressed the law of God, Christ was to fulfill every requirement of that law, and thus show perfect obedience. "Lo, I come to do thy will, O God!" Christ honored the ordinance of baptism by submitting to this rite. In this act he identified himself with his people as their representative and head. As their substitute, he takes upon him their sins, numbering himself with the transgressors, taking the steps the sinner is required to take, and doing the work the sinner must do. (*The Spirit of Prophecy*, vol. 2, 60)

In this assumed type of the Messiah, Daniel was given the prophecy of the 70 weeks, a prophecy dealing with the intercessory work of Christ. This prophecy states that the Jewish people had 490 years to finish the transgression (finish their rebellion), make an end of sin (be victorious over sin), make reconciliation for iniquity (ministry of reconciliation), bring in everlasting righteousness, (show what righteousness is), seal up the vision and prophecy (complete the prophecy of 70 weeks), and anoint the most holy place (open up the heavenly sanctuary).

The prophecy goes on to show that during this time, the city, temple, street, and walls of the desolate city Jerusalem were to be rebuilt. Christ fulfilled the entire 70-week prophecy by His work at Calvary and beyond. At Calvary, the rebellion was finished for all who come to the cross and cease their war against God. At Calvary, victory over sin was accomplished, for therein is the power of Christ to die to self. At Calvary, the ministry of reconciliation is perfectly demonstrated through His sacrifice for us. There everlasting righteousness is ushered in because there we receive it exchange for our sins, and there the prophecy finds it completion and the way to the heavenly sanctuary is opened.

However, He did more than this. He rebuilt the temple at Calvary. "Jesus answered and said unto them, Destroy this temple, and in three days I will raise it up. Then said the Jews, Forty and six years was this temple in building, and wilt thou rear it up in three days? But he spake of the temple of his body" (John 2:19–21). He established his church, the spiritual city of Israel at Calvary.

"I say also unto thee, That thou art Peter, and upon this rock I will build my church; and the gates of hell shall not prevail against it" (Matthew 16:18). At Calvary he built the street (or way) to salvation "even in troublous times" (Daniel 9:25), saying "I, if I be lifted up from the earth, will draw all men unto me" (John 12:32). "Jesus saith unto him, I am the way, the truth, and the life: no man cometh unto the Father, but by me" (John 14:6).

Also, just as Nehemiah refused to "come down" because he was doing a "great work" and completed his work fifty-two days later, so fifty-two days after Christ showed that He would not "come down" for He too was "doing a great work," a wall of fire went up around the church on the day of Pentecost. At that same time, Christ opened up the way into the heavenly sanctuary. He "caused the sacrifices and oblations to cease" at the cross while "confirming the covenant with many" through His sacrifice.

The Cross and Daniel 11

As stated before, Daniel 11:22 points to the breaking, or crucifixion, of the "prince of the covenant." Any assault upon the covenant is an assault upon its Prince. Later, Daniel 11:32 states, "Such as do wickedly against the covenant shall he corrupt by flatteries: but the people that do know their God shall be strong, and do exploits." To reject the covenant is equated with not knowing God. Daniel 11:44 points out that the tidings will ultimately bring about the final moments in earth's history. These glad tidings of the Christ and Him crucified in connection with the three angels' messages will bring about the final destruction of the antichrist.

The Cross and Daniel 12

Daniel 12 points several times to the cross of Christ. First in Daniel 12:1, we find the following, "at that time thy people shall be delivered, every one that shall be found written in the book." This book is "the book of life of the Lamb slain from the foundation of the world" (see Revelation 13:8). Only those who have accepted the sacrifice, the cross of Christ, and allowed it to do its work of cleansing sin from their lives will come up out of the graves unto "everlasting life" (Daniel 12:2).

Daniel 12:3 references those who are wise, turning many to righteousness. Who are these wise ones? And what is this wisdom? Paul wrote, "We preach Christ crucified, unto the Jews a stumbling block, and unto the Greeks foolishness; but unto them which are called, both Jews and Greeks, Christ the power of God, and the wisdom of God" (1 Corinthians 1:23, 24). Through the preaching of the cross in connection with the three angels' messages, God's people will turn many to the righteousness of Christ as their only hope of eternal salvation.

Daniel 12:4 tells us that at the time of the end "knowledge shall be increased." This increasing knowledge is revealed in Habakkuk 2:14: "The earth shall be filled with the knowledge of the glory of the Lord, as the waters cover the sea." The increasing knowledge is that of the glory of the Lord, the same glory of Revelation 18:1—the glory of the cross (Galatians 6:14).

Daniel 12:10 notes that many will be "purified" and made "white." The cleansing of the sanctuary is the time when the saints of God are to be purified and made white by the blood of the Lamb (see Revelation 7:14). It is the final blotting out of their sins that prepares them for the second coming of Christ. This cleansing work can be done only in light of the cross, and its real purpose in the life of a Christian.

As God's people begin to lift up the cross of Christ, it will indeed draw His people, His sincere people unto Him. As God's people, may we be known, not as legalists, but as people of the cross, lifting high Christ and Him crucified as the evidence and proof of our faith and the certainty of the three angels' messages. Then the earth will be filled with knowledge of the glory of the Lord as the waters cover the sea.

Group Project

1. Elaborate on each section.
2. How is the cross related to the prophecies of Daniel?
3. How can we make the cross the center of our evangelistic seminars and Bible studies?

Chapter 21
The Cross-centered
Prophecies of Revelation

From the book of Daniel we turn our attention to the book of Revelation. This chapter is dedicated to looking at the prophecies of this book in the new light of the old rugged cross.

The Cross and Revelation 1–3

Revelation 1:5 says, "Unto him that loved us, and washed us from our sins in his own blood." This is the grand theme of the book of Revelation. It is a depiction of the war of Jesus to cleanse us by His blood, and Satan's counter assault to keep us defiled with sin. The first three chapters of Revelation is an address to the seven churches.

Jesus spoke to each of these churches, laying out the conflict before them. His closing statement to each of the seven churches includes these words, "to him that overcometh" (see Revelation 2:7, 11, 17, 26; 3:5, 12, 21). Revelation 12:11 tells us *how* every soul in these seven churches would overcome: "They overcame him by the blood of the Lamb, and by the word of their testimony; and they loved not their lives unto the death." Only those who allow the cross to do its cleansing work will overcome the antagonistic forces of darkness. Thus, the cross is the true center of the messages contained in Revelation's first three chapters.

Interestingly, Revelation 3:20 says, "Behold, I stand at the door, and knock: if any man hear my voice, and open the door, I will come in to him, and will sup with him, and he with me." This message is directed to the church of Laodicea. God's last-day church is said to be in a place where its people feel they are rich and increased with goods (verse 17). God's church has been secure in its doctrinal teachings, and we feel that we have everything we need. However, Jesus says, "I have one more thing for you. I want to come in and sup with you."

What is the meal of which we are invited to partake? Jesus himself tells us, "Verily, verily, I say unto you, Except ye eat the flesh of the Son of man, and drink his blood, ye have no life in you" (John 6:53). The meal that we so desperately need as a church is the very sacrifice of Christ.

> As they were eating, Jesus took bread, and blessed it, and brake it, and gave it to the disciples, and said, Take, eat; this is my body. And he took the cup, and gave thanks, and gave it to them, saying,

Drink ye all of it; For this is my blood of the new testament, which is shed for many for the remission of sins. (Matthew 26:26–28)

We are missing the sacrifice of Christ in our temple. The chief Cornerstone of our preaching is still laying out in the streets. Christ knocks because He wants be a part of our temple, not just any part, the chief Cornerstone.

The Cross and Revelation 4, 5

The throne-room scene of Revelation, chapters four and five, focus around the Lamb who was slain (Revelation 5:6) but is now alive. Only Christ is found worthy to open the seals that are closely tied with the destiny of humanity. He is worthy because he "was slain." (Revelation 5:9). Again, His sacrifice is the theme of these chapters.

The Cross and Revelation 6

Revelation 6:2 speaks of a rider on a white horse, which is a reference to Jesus working through the early church and conquering hearts through the preaching message of the cross, "Christ crucified" (1 Corinthians 1:23), the Lamb slain for our sins. In like manner, the martyrs who followed in the steps of Lamb and were "slain" will be given white robes (Revelation 6:11). Their blood will be avenged because they have the same blood "of the Lamb." Those who persecute them actually persecute Jesus. The chapter closes with the terrifying scene that all who have rejected and warred against the blood of Lamb must face the wrath of the Lamb.

The Cross and Revelation 7

Revelation 7:3 speaks of the sealing of God's people: "Saying, Hurt not the earth, neither the sea, nor the trees, till we have sealed the servants of our God in their foreheads." The servants of God are sealed; the four winds are not loosed until they are all sealed. Then probation closes.

Later in this verse we are told how they made it through the time of trouble. "These are they which came out of great tribulation, and have washed their robes, and made them white in the blood of the Lamb" (Revelation 7:14). The redeemed washed their robes in the blood of the Lamb, synonymous with being sealed. Only those who have allowed the blood to cleanse them from lawbreaking, including the Sabbath commandment, will be sealed by the seal of God.

The Cross and Revelation 10

Revelation 10 is a reference to the great disappointment of 1844. As a church, we experienced a bitter disappointment. In misunderstanding the prophecy of the 2,300 years and its connected message of "the Bridegroom cometh," the book of Daniel, which was at first sweet to the mouth, became bitter to the belly. But this message, "the Bridegroom cometh," was again to be given to the world, no longer in bitterness, but in zeal and passion the sweetness of the message was to go forth.

> The angel of Revelation 10 is represented as having one foot on the sea and one foot on the land, showing that the message will be carried to distant lands, the ocean will be crossed, and the islands of the sea will hear the proclamation of the last message of warning to our world. (*Selected Messages*, Book 2, 107, 108)

This book which was eaten containing the words of God, the book of Daniel, is reminiscent of the sweet bread, heavenly manna. "The house of Israel called the name thereof Manna: and it was like coriander seed, white; and the taste of it was like wafers made with honey" (Exodus 16:31). Of this manna, Jesus said:

> Your fathers did eat manna in the wilderness, and are dead. This is the bread which cometh down from heaven, that a man may eat thereof, and not die. I am the living bread which came down from heaven: if any man eat of this bread, he shall live for ever: and the bread that I will give is my flesh, which I will give for the life of the world. (John 6:49–51)

The sacrifice of Christ is the "sweet bread" of life that we must take to the world—Christ lifted up. His sacrifice is the great center of our message. Without the cross of Christ, our message may indeed be received as only "bitterness." "How sweet are thy words unto my taste! yea, sweeter than honey to my mouth!" (Psalm 119:103). The cross, indeed, is the sweetness of our message, the power of the book of Daniel. Rightly understood, what sincere Christian can resist?

The Cross and Revelation 11:19

"The temple of God was opened in heaven, and there was seen in his temple the ark of his testament" (Revelation 11:19). As Seventh-day Adventists, we have rightly pointed to the fact that the ark of the testament contains the Ten Commandments.

> The ark in the tabernacle on earth contained the two tables of stone, upon which were inscribed the precepts of the law of God. The ark was merely a receptacle for the tables of the law, and the

presence of these divine precepts gave to it its value and sacredness. When the temple of God was opened in heaven, the ark of His testament was seen. Within the holy of holies, in the sanctuary in heaven, the divine law is sacredly enshrined—the law that was spoken by God Himself amid the thunders of Sinai and written with His own finger on the tables of stone. (*The Great Controversy*, 433, 434)

This should strike fear in the heart of any human being, for none of us can be found righteous enough to pass the test by our own attempts to keep the law. What hope is there for us?

Let us not forget that inside the ark was also Aaron's rod that budded. Aaron's budding rod was a sign of death and resurrection. A rod is a dead stick, but the rod budded—came to life—and gave Aaron the right to be high priest (see the full story in Numbers 17). In like manner, Jesus has earned the right to be our high priest because He died, came to life, and has ascended into heaven. Along with drawing attention to the law of God, we must remember to point out our crucified and risen High Priest who is able to save us unto the uttermost, represented by that living Stick. In Him is our hope. "Which hope we have as an anchor of the soul, both sure and stedfast, and which entereth into that within the veil; whither the forerunner is for us entered, even Jesus, made an high priest for ever" (Hebrews 6:19, 20).

Manna was also found in the ark, of which Christ Himself said is a symbol of His sacrifice. "I am the living bread which came down from heaven: if any man eat of this bread, he shall live for ever: and the bread that I will give is my flesh, *which I will give for the life of the world*" (John 6:51, emphasis added). Thus, the contents of the ark all point to Christ's work on the cross. The message that directs our minds into the most holy place is to signify to us that we can only be forgiven as we go to the One who died because of our transgressions, and that as we eat of his flesh and drink of his blood, He will empower us to be victorious over sin and live forever. Christ said to the Jews in his day, "Your fathers did eat manna in the wilderness, and are dead. This is the bread which cometh down from heaven, that a man may eat thereof, and not die" (John 6:49, 50). So the message now is all who partake of that heavenly manna will indeed live forever.

The Cross and Revelation 12

The history of the Dark Ages is shown in this chapter. The true church of God, fleeing from persecution, is depicted as hiding in the wilderness. "The woman fled into the wilderness, where she hath a place prepared of God, that they should feed her there a thousand two hundred and threescore days" (Revelation 12:6). What is the food that sustained her during this time? Christ and Him crucified, the bread and wine of the covenant (see Matthew 26:26–28; John 5:53). Of the church in hiding and the last-day church it is written, "They overcame him by the blood of the Lamb, and by the word of their testimony; and they loved not their lives unto the death" (Revelation 12:11). Christ died for them, they copied the principle of the cross in being willing to lay down their lives for the truth.

The Cross and Revelation 13

Revelation 13 covers the beast from the sea, the beast from the earth, and the mark of the first beast. Each of these elements centers its attack on the cross of Christ and the covenant established at Calvary.

The sea beast, representing the papacy, will be thought to be of God because of its apparent resurrection from a wound unto death. Just as Christ was wounded unto death, then resurrected so that many wondered after Him, and believed on Him, so the sea beast that received a deadly wound will also undergo a resurrection of power, which will lead the deceived to wonder after it, claiming it to be of God. "All that dwell upon the earth shall worship him, whose names are not written in the book of life of the Lamb slain from the foundation of the world" (Revelation 13:8).

The pivotal issue is having one's name written in the Lamb's book of life. To have his or her name written there, a person needs to worship none other than the worthy One who was slain at the cross. The principle of the cross, of self denial, leads him or her to prefer persecution and death rather than worship the beast, even with a threat of death.

In fact, death has no power over God's obedient ones. To remain in the book of the Lamb "that was slain," they too must be willing to be slain, to die daily, and if need be, to have a willingness to lay down their lives unto actual death like the three Hebrews before the image of Babylon. These three men chose to suffer in the fires of persecution with the Lamb by their side rather than deny Him and worship another in order to live temporal and temporary lives.

The beast "from the earth," apostate Protestantism, also seek to imitate the work of the Lamb "I beheld another beast coming up out of the earth; and he had two horns like a lamb, and he spake as a dragon" (Revelation 13:11). Just as the true Lamb rose out of the "heart of the earth" (see Matthew 12:40 for the sign of Jonah) after a period of three days and nights, so this lamblike beast rose out of the earth after a prophetic period of three and half times (see Daniel 7:25).

Just as the true Lamb, after rising out of the earth, brought fire down from heaven in the sight of men (Acts 2:1–3), so this counterfeit lamb like beast will make "fire come down from heaven on the earth in the sight of men" (Revelation 13:13) after he arises out of the earth, signaling a counterfeit revival with a false spirit.

As we know, the mark of the beast, is simply a counterfeit of the seal of God, which is the character of Christ fixed in the forehead of his saints. "The seal of the living God will be placed upon those only who bear a likeness to Christ in character" (*Child Guidance*, 182).

How is this character fixed in the mind? "Thou wilt keep him in perfect peace, whose mind is stayed on thee: because he trusteth in thee" (Isaiah 26:3).

> Let this mind be in you, which was also in Christ Jesus: who, being in the form of God, thought it not robbery to be equal with God: but made himself of no reputation, and took upon him the form of a servant, and was made in the likeness of men: and being found in fashion as a man, he humbled himself, and became obedient unto death, even the death of the cross. (Philippians 2:5–8)

This is why only the "servants" are sealed. They became servants because they fixed their minds upon Christ who "took upon the form of a servant" and demonstrated true servant-hood as revealed by His actions upon the cross. By beholding Christ "lifted up," the five wise virgins were sealed with his character and avoided the mark. The Sabbath, the sign of rest, was kept by Christ at Calvary—He rested, even in his death. This affirmation at Calvary of resting on the Sabbath, *even unto death*, is *seared and sealed* in the minds of His people. They will be like Him at all costs, even unto the death decree.

The Cross and Revelation 18

As mentioned before, the glory and power of the angel of Revelation 18:1 points to the cross. It is also crucial to see that it is the cross is the power that will draw people by the thousands out of Babylon. Says the Scripture, "Come out of her, my people, that ye be not partakers of her sins, and that ye receive not of her plagues" (Revelation 18:4).

The issue of Revelation 18 is the issue of sin. When Jesus comes, who will be found with the stains of Babylon's sins upon their garments? Only one detergent can cleanse the soul from the sin-stained garment, and that is the blood of Christ. The call *out of* Babylon is also a call *to* Calvary.

> When the mind is drawn to the cross of Calvary, Christ by imperfect sight is discerned on the shameful cross. Why did He

die? In consequence of sin. What is sin? The transgression of the law. Then the eyes are open to see the character of sin. The law is broken but cannot pardon the transgressor. It is our schoolmaster, condemning to punishment. Where is the remedy? The law drives us to Christ, who was hanged upon the cross that He might be able to impart His righteousness to fallen, sinful man and thus present men to His Father in His righteous character.

Christ on the cross not only draws men to repentance toward God for the transgression of His law—for whom God pardons He first makes penitent—but Christ has satisfied Justice; He has proffered Himself as an atonement. His gushing blood, His broken body, satisfy the claims of the broken law, and thus He bridges the gulf which sin has made. He suffered in the flesh, that with His bruised and broken body He might cover the defenseless sinner. The victory gained at His death on Calvary broke forever the accusing power of Satan over the universe and silenced his charges that self-denial was impossible with God and therefore not essential in the human family. (*Selected Messages*, Book 1, 341)

Those who remain in Babylon are those who deny the cleansing power of the cross. Their sins remain upon them, and they must ultimately be destroyed with Babylon.

The Cross and Revelation 19

Revelation 19 points to the coming of Christ. "I saw heaven opened, and behold a white horse; and he that sat upon him was called Faithful and True, and in righteousness he doth judge and make war. His eyes were as a flame of fire, and on his head were many crowns; and he had a name written, that no man knew, but he himself. And he was clothed with a vesture dipped in blood: and his name is called The Word of God. And the armies which were in heaven followed him upon white horses, clothed in fine linen, white and clean" (Revelation 19:11–14).

Notice that he comes with a garment dipped in blood. This is the sign He is looking for, the special clothing that His people will also be wearing when He comes. Those who have washed their robes in the blood of the Lamb will see Christ's vesture dipped in blood and will be overjoyed at the sight. They are identified with the Lamb and His sacrifice having lived it out in their own lives.

The Cross and Revelation 20

"Blessed and holy is he that hath part in the first resurrection: on such the second death hath no power, but they shall be priests of God and of Christ, and shall reign with him a thousand years" (Revelation 20:6). Here, the Bible speaks of God's redeemed reigning for a thousand years as kings and priests (see Revelation 5:10).

They became such, however, by the blood or the cross of Christ. "From Jesus Christ, who is the faithful witness, and the first begotten of the dead, and the prince of the kings of the earth. Unto him that loved us, and washed us from our sins in his own blood, and hath made us kings and priests unto God and his Father; to him be glory and dominion for ever and ever. Amen" (Revelation 1:5, 6). Only those who truly accept the cross, and its cleansing power from lawlessness, will make it to the heavenly realms during the thousand years. Those who were "not found written in the book of life" (Revelation 20:15), in essence, rejected the slain Lamb and His work in their lives.

The Cross and Revelation 21

Revelation 21 is a beautiful description of the New Jerusalem. However, "there shall in no wise enter into it any thing that defileth, neither whatsoever worketh abomination, or maketh a lie: but they which are written in the Lamb's book of life" (Revelation 21:27).

Again, the blood is the deciding factor between those who enter and those who cannot. It is by the blood that we enter into the Lamb's book of life, by the blood that we are cleansed and purified. Therefore, those who are unclean, having rejected the work of the blood in their lives, can in no wise enter into the city.

Verse four records that there will be no more death. This is because Christ, "through death," destroyed "him that had the power of death, that is, the devil" (Hebrews 2:14). As result of Christ's death, not only has Satan been destroyed (chapter 20), but "the last enemy that shall be destroyed is death" (1 Corinthians 15:26).

Verse 6 records the words, "It is done." Just as Jesus cried these words when He accomplished His mission on the cross, so He will again say these words, demonstrating that all things are made new, in actuality because of what was "finished" at the cross. It speaks of the water of life being given freely. That water began to flow at Calvary through Christ's pierced side (see John 19:34). "In that day there shall be a fountain opened to the house of David and to the inhabitants of Jerusalem for sin and for uncleanness" (Zechariah 13:1).

The Cross and Revelation 22

The summation of Revelation points once more to the cross. The tree of life is depicted in heaven. "Blessed are they that do his commandments, that they may have right to the tree of life, and may enter in through the gates into the city" (Revelation 22:14).

Only those who have eaten from the tree of life here on earth will be able to eat of tree of life in heaven. What is the earthly tree of life? Nothing but the old rugged cross—the tree upon which Christ, the sweet manna and the first-fruits of God, was hung for our sins. Except we eat of His flesh and His blood here on earth, we can never taste of tree of life in heaven.

As God's people learn to focus upon the cross, an incredible power will attend the preaching of the three angels' messages. May that light that is to lighten the earth be accepted by the people of God.

Group Project and Question

1. What impacted you the most about this chapter?

2. How is the cross related to the prophecies of Revelation?

3. Why should we teach this book, centered on Christ and His sacrifice?

Chapter 22
The Cross-centered Fundamental Beliefs of Seventh-day Adventism

I n this chapter, we will look at the distinctive teachings of our faith in the new light of the old rugged cross. Presenting the cross as the center, and not only the bookends of our tenets of faith will give the proper view of the gospel for those looking for Christ-centered truth.

It will be seen from this chapter that Satan has been busy perverting the meaning of the cross, warring against it through false teachings and doctrines. He has even gone so far as to use the cross against the cross, and many well meaning Christians have thus fallen for a counterfeit meaning of the cross.

The following chapters are not meant to be an exhaustive study of our teachings. It is presupposed that as a Seventh-day Adventist you have an understanding of these topics. Therefore, we will only focus on the added element of the cross.

The Cross and the Israel

> But now in Christ Jesus ye who sometimes were far off are made nigh by the blood of Christ. For he is our peace, who hath made both one, and hath broken down the middle wall of partition between us. (Ephesians 2:13, 14; see also Galatians 3:29)

The death of Christ destroyed the middle wall partition between the Jews and Gentiles. The teaching, therefore, that God has a special plan for the literal children of Israel that is separate from the Gentile and that there is a wall of separation upheld by the Bible itself is an anti-cross, thus anti-Christ, teaching. This teaching denies the work that was accomplished at the cross (see Romans 2:28, 29; Galatians 3:7, 27–29). Our appeal at the end of a message like this should be an appeal to accept the cross as it relates to the issue of Israel.

The Cross and the Temple

In the book of Daniel we are given a striking prophecy concerning the temple in Israel.

He shall confirm the covenant with many for one week: and in the midst of the week he shall cause the sacrifice and the oblation to cease, and for the overspreading of abominations he shall make it desolate, even until the consummation, and that determined shall be poured upon the desolate. (Daniel 9:27)

Because of the "overspreading of abominations," namely the rejection of the Messiah's sacrifice, we are told that the temple of Israel, the literal building, would become "desolate, even until the consummation," or the end of all things. The cross of Christ opened the way into the heavenly sanctuary, putting an end to the need to use an earthly temple. Therefore, to teach and believe that an earthly temple in Jerusalem where sacrifices are reinstated has any spiritual significance or is a part of God's end-time plan is a direct denial of the cross of Christ and a contradiction of the prophecy of Daniel. Our appeal to our friends should be to accept the cross as it relates to the issue of the temple.

The Cross and the Rapture

The erroneous rapture theory teaches that the people of God will not be present during the great tribulation, and that those who have accepted the cross will escape tribulation. This is an affront to the principle of the cross. We do not escape tribulation by the cross; instead, we learn to endure.

Beloved, think it not strange concerning the fiery trial which is to try you, as though some strange thing happened unto you: But rejoice, inasmuch as ye are partakers of Christ's sufferings; that, when his glory shall be revealed, ye may be glad also with exceeding joy. (1 Peter 4:12, 13)

The principle of the cross is endurance, not exemption. Thousands of Christians have been led to accept a counterfeit cross. They have then been led to believe that they need not prepare for tribulation or to face the mark of the beast, the image, etc. Christ Himself warned of pending tribulation when he said, "If they have persecuted me, they will also persecute you" (John 15:20).

Only those who are armed with the cross will make it through the great tribulation. Our appeal to our friends should be to reject the false "exemption principle" to the cross, and in its place accept and expect tribulation because of the cross.

The Cross and Immortality

The teaching that man is naturally immortal is another affront to the cross. John 3:16 tells us: "For God so loved the world, that he gave his only begotten Son, that whosoever believeth in him should not perish, but have everlasting life." Immortality, eternal life, is given only to those who accept the cross. The teaching that we naturally have immortality, in essence, tells the world that the cross is not the only way to life.

We are told that Jesus *died* on the cross. The cross, therefore, proves what death really is. If death is not really death, then Jesus did not really die. If death is simply a transition from one world to another, from one form of existence to another, that would mean that Jesus died when He left heaven to come to earth in the form of a man. Foolish as this is sounds, it makes sense if death simply means transition from one form to another.

Moreover, Jesus did not transition anywhere when He died, not heaven, not hell. He died. If He did not truly die, then the cross was a hoax. If he did not truly die, then we are all still in our sins for no penalty was paid on our behalf. The cross proves that the dead are neither in heaven nor in hell. Our appeal on this subject should be an appeal to accept the cross as the only way to eternal life, a gift given when Jesus comes again, and to accept the cross as it relates to the subject of death.

The Cross and Hellfire

The cross proves the fallacy of the doctrine of an eternally burning hellfire. Jesus paid the full penalty of the sins of the world. This no Christian will argue. In fact, if Jesus did not pay the full penalty for our sins, humanity would be lost. The question for our friends in the various churches is this: "Are the wages of sin death or eternal torment?"

Most Christians would probably answer that the wages of sin is eternal torment. Then how and when did Jesus pay this penalty? He was dead for three days. Either he got a major discount from the penalty of sin, in which case all humanity is lost, or the wages of sin is death, a price that Jesus did, in fact, pay.

The Bible tells us: "All we like sheep have gone astray; we have turned every one to his own way; and the Lord hath laid on him the iniquity of us all" (Isaiah 53:6). The Contemporary English Version reads, "All of us were like sheep that had wandered off. We had each gone our own way, but the Lord gave him the punishment we deserved."

The punishment that we deserved, He suffered. Until it can be proven that Christ suffered and is still suffering right now, the case for eternal torment stands refuted by the cross of Christ.

Furthermore, if the wicked burn forever, it must necessarily put them in heaven forever since the location of the torment of the wicked is "in the presence of the Lamb." "He [the wicked] shall be tormented with fire and brimstone in the presence of the holy angels, and *in the presence of the Lamb*" (Revelation 14:10, emphasis added). If the wicked are not destroyed in the presence of the Lamb, they must eventually find themselves in the midst of the throne, where the Lamb will dwell with His people. This is fallacy. Only by the cross can we dwell in the presence of the Lamb forever (see Revelation 5:6; 7:17).

The Cross and the Law

When the sinner looks upon the cross, he sees there the dying Savior. The question comes to mind, "Why does this Man suffer? What was His crime?" That sinner soon learns that this Man has decided of His own free will to suffer in his or her place.

> He is despised and rejected of men; a man of sorrows, and acquainted with grief: and we hid as it were our faces from him; he was despised, and we esteemed him not. Surely he hath borne our griefs, and carried our sorrows: yet we did esteem him stricken, smitten of God, and afflicted. But he was wounded for our transgressions, he was bruised for our iniquities: the chastisement of our peace was upon him; and with his stripes we are healed. All we like sheep have gone astray; we have turned every one to his own way; and the Lord hath laid on him the iniquity of us all. He was oppressed, and he was afflicted, yet he opened not his mouth: he is brought as a lamb to the slaughter, and as a sheep before her shearers is dumb, so he openeth not his mouth. (Isaiah 53:3–7)

An amazing truth is here revealed. Christ died because of our sins. The gospel is designed to rid the entire universe of the very thing that killed Christ. God was faced with a decision. He could have eliminated the whole human race and thus spared His Son's life. But "God so loved the world, that he gave his only begotten Son, that whosoever believeth in him should not perish, but have everlasting life" (John 3:16). Between destroying the human race and giving His Son, God chose to give His Son. What amazing love! The cross of Christ establishes forever the love of God for humanity.

There was another option. God could have also decided to get rid of the law that declared man guilty: "for where no law is, there is no transgression" (Romans 4:15). Would God get rid of the law in order to free guilty man? The reality is that God would no more get rid of His law to save us than we would get rid of the law against murder in order to make murderers innocent.

"God spared not the angels that sinned, but cast them down to hell, and delivered them into chains of darkness, to be reserved unto judgment" (2 Peter 2:4). Remember, "sin is the transgression of the law" (1 John 3:4). We are told in 2 Peter that the angels "sinned." Between the law of God and His angels that persisted in transgressing that law, God, instead of yielding His law, which is the very transcript of His character, put the angels out of heaven.

"'He that spared not his own Son, but delivered him up for us all, how shall he not with him also freely give us all things?'" (Romans 8:32). God "spared not his own Son." From what? He spared not His Son from the penalty of the law: "For the wages of sin is death" (Romans 6:23). Between the law of God and His very own Son, God "spared not" His very own Son; instead, God allowed Him to die rather than to abolish His law and its penalty. This is the greatest evidence for the immutability of the cross.

The cross proves the permanency of the law of God. If God spared not His own Son from the penalty of the law (of which He was not personally guilty), what makes us think that He will spare those who openly and willfully transgress or ignore the commandments?

What *did* God get rid of at the cross? Our guilt—at cross we are justified, forgiven. The cross demonstrates that God loves us so much that He gave up His Son. It also demonstrates that God's law is so important that He would not alter it in any way or do away with it, not even to spare His own Son. Also, lest it be seen that man or the law was more important than His Son, we are told that only through accepting the sacrifice of His Son can we hope for eternal life. It all points back to the sacrifice of Christ.

> As the sinner looks upon the Saviour dying on Calvary, and realizes that the Sufferer is divine, he asks why, this great sacrifice was made; and the cross points to the holy law of God, which has been transgressed. The death of Christ is an unanswerable argument to the immutability and righteousness of the law. (*The Bible Echo*, March 15, 1893, emphasis added)

The Cross and the New Covenant

The cross is God's proposal to mankind. "For God so loved the world, that he gave his only begotten Son, that whosoever believeth in him should not perish, but have everlasting life" (John 3:16). God's view of the covenant is that of a marriage, the exchanging of wedding vows:

Behold, the days come, saith the Lord, that I will make a new covenant with the house of Israel, and with the house of Judah: Not according to the covenant that I made with their fathers in the day that I took them by the hand to bring them out of the land of Egypt; which my covenant they brake, although I was an husband unto them, saith the Lord: But this shall be the covenant that I will make with the house of Israel; After those days, saith the Lord, I will put my law in their inward parts, and write it in their hearts; and will be their God, and they shall be my people. (Jeremiah 31:31–33)

Like a husband, God took Israel by the hand, but they broke His covenant. At the cross, Christ proposed to humanity. It was the proposal to again take His hand, to join Him in a covenant relationship, a proposal to live forever with Him. The cross is the wooing of humanity to Christ. "I, if I be lifted up from the earth, will draw all men unto me" (John 12:32). Many Christians have said yes to the proposal, but saying yes to a proposal does not make the pair married. Marriage occurs only after the exchanging of the wedding vows.

Those wedding vows are the Ten Commandments, written on our hearts and in our minds (see Hebrews 8:8–10). Jesus said, "This cup is the new testament in my blood, which is shed for you" (Luke 22:20). In other words, His death, His sacrifice confirmed, sealed, and reveals the worth of the marriage covenant, the wedding vows. To reject the Ten Commandments, or any part of the whole, is to reject the proposal the cross extends, and thus the cross itself.

This covenant seen as the exchanging of wedding vows reveals the fallacy of the argument that the cross makes us no longer "bound by the law," and that Christians by it are set free from obeying the law. Christians who feel that keeping the commandments robs them of their "freedom in grace" are equivalent to a man who feels that the rules of marriage are too restrictive, robbing him of the freedom to see other women. While there are rules and boundaries in marriage, those who are in love with one another do not see these as rules. Their vows were not only written on paper, but they were also written on their hearts.

Freedom to those who are in love is imprisonment to those who are not. Likewise, to those who truly love Jesus and accept the cross, the Ten Commandments are freedom, peace, and joy. Like David, they can say, "I hate vain thoughts: but thy law do I love" (Psalm 119:113). To those who merely claim to love Jesus, the law is drudgery and bondage. "For to be carnally minded is death; but to be spiritually minded is life and peace. Because the carnal mind is enmity against God: for it is not subject to the law of God, neither indeed can be. So then they that are in the flesh cannot please God" (Romans 8:6–8). Thus, Jesus said, "If ye love me, keep my commandments" (John 14:15).

Revelation 17:5 depicts Babylon and her daughters as harlots: "upon her forehead was a name written, MYSTERY, BABYLON THE GREAT, THE MOTHER OF HARLOTS AND ABOMINATIONS OF THE EARTH." A harlot is called so because she makes no commitment to one person. She is unwilling to be bound by the rules of marriage. The harlot represents a system that while professing to say "yes" to the proposal made by Christ at the cross, refuses to abide by the wedding vows that follow. Jesus put it this way: "Ye hypocrites, well did Esaias prophesy of you, saying, This people draweth nigh unto me with their mouth, and honoureth me with their lips; but their heart is far from me. But in vain they do worship me, teaching for doctrines the commandments of men" (Matthew15:7–9).

Notice that these people draw near to Christ. How? With their lips—they profess to have been drawn by the "drawing" power of the cross. They said "yes" to the proposal in theory. Yet in their hearts, the place where the law of God (the wedding vows) are to be written, they refuse to take to the cross. Why? The cross is about total submission, total commitment.

Imagine the bride or the bridegroom questioning the meaning of the vows, denying some parts of the vows while accepting others. This would be a travesty, a sure sign of a doomed marriage and a heartbreaking embarrassment to the other person. Yet many Christians today either ignore the Ten Commandments altogether or seek to find ways around obeying them, the fourth vow in particular. Presenting the new covenant as the wedding vows in connection with the proposal of the cross to our friends in the fallen systems will strike a chord of response in those who genuinely "love" God. They will come out of Babylon, the non-committal power, and be joined to God in a true covenant relationship.

The Cross and Our Health and Lifestyle Message

Satan has even found a way to take the cross, which was meant to cleanse us from sin, and use it to sanction defiling the temple of God. Most Christians believe that the cross of Christ set them free to eat anything they want, and they do not see that Peter's vision was about the cleansing of humanity by the cross. The cross cleanses every area of our lives. It matters not how, but Satan will find a way to desecrate what God desires to make and keep clean. Therefore, every effort to defile the body through food and substances, and the mind through entertainment, is an attack upon the cross. The health message, we have been told is "the right arm" of the everlasting gospel, the third angel's message.

The health reform is as closely related to the third angel's message as the arm to the body; but the arm cannot take the place of the body. The proclamation of the third angel's message, the commandments of God, and the testimony of Jesus is the great burden of our work. The message is to be proclaimed with a loud cry, and is to go to the whole world. The presentation of health principles must be united with this message, but must not in any case be independent of it, or in any way take the place of it. (*Counsels to Writers and Editors*, 139)

So how is the health message intimately tied in the three angel's messages? The number one cause of death in America, as well as the world, is spiritual *heart disease*. "The wages of sin is death" (Romans 6:23). This Scripture verse points us to the fact that most *diseases* begin because of breaking the law of God.

Ellen White wrote, "Few realize the power that the mind has over the body. A great deal of the sickness which afflicts humanity has its origin in the mind and can only be cured by restoring the mind to health" (*Testimonies for the Church*, vol. 3, 184). "The mind needs to be controlled, for it has a most powerful influence upon the health" (*Testimonies for the Church*, vol. 2, 523). She also recorded, "Sickness of the mind prevails everywhere. Nine tenths of the diseases from which men suffer have their foundation here" (*Testimonies for the Church*, 444). How is this so?

When Eve sinned by eating the forbidden fruit, we are told, "she felt the sensation of a new and more exalted life ... she felt no ill effects from eating the fruit, nothing which could be interpreted to mean death, but, instead, a pleasurable sensation, which she imagined was as the angels felt" (*Counsels on Health*, 108, 109).

This feeling was brought on by the risk she had just taken. Something flooded her body giving her that pleasurable feeling. In today's terminology we would call that an "adrenaline rush"—an exciting, pleasurable effect produced when the adrenal glands dump a large dose of adrenaline into the bloodstream. The adrenaline rush usually occurs when the body senses danger, duress, stress, distress, also known as the "fight-or-flight" moment. The heart rate increases, pleasure-giving endorphins are released by the pituitary gland, and the breathing rate ramps up. The result of all this extra oxygen, energy, and hormones is the "adrenaline high," a euphoric feeling that can last for hours. The sudden flood of adrenaline also temporarily shuts down the immune system to conserve energy for survival.[11]

11 Julia Layton, "How Fear Works," http://science.howstuffworks.com/environmental/life/inside-the-mind/fear2.htm.

These adrenal glands were designed to warn us of danger, which is a good thing. But when we are under constant stress, the adrenal system stays turned on. The result is that the body receives large and constant amounts of adrenaline that in turn impairs the immune system, creating a toxic environment in the body. Scientists are only now discovering that stress, which releases an overproduction of adrenaline *and begins in the mind*, is the underlying cause of cancer, heart disease, stroke, diabetes, Crohn's disease, multiple sclerosis, obesity, anxiety, crime, pornography, drug abuse, depression, addiction, and more.[12]

Bearing this in mind, the root of all stress is the breaking of God's law, either by ourselves, those we love, or even by those we don't know. Think of man or woman breaking the seventh commandment concerning adultery. Think of the fear and stress it puts the guilty party under and the amount of adrenaline being released in the body as a result. When crimes are committed in a neighborhood it leaves the innocent in a state of stress, worried for their safety. Our loved ones cause us stress when the live dangerously. Our adrenaline-crazed society goes from one rush to the next, not realizing that the exhilarating sense of sin committed by either ourselves or those around us—or the poisonous emotions of lust, anger, and resentment—are quite literally killing us. Every negative thought releases a dose of adrenaline into the body. Doctors call it chronic stress syndrome.

Even our diet can flood our system with adrenaline. Caffeine and alcohol are both diuretics, meaning that they dehydrate the cells. When the cells are dehydrated, the body reacts as though it is in danger, releasing adrenaline into the blood stream. This is why coffee drinkers drink coffee to "stay alert." That alert feeling comes from the adrenaline release as a result of the body being in duress.[13]

When animals sense they are about to be slaughtered, their bodies release the fight-or-flight chemical into the blood stream. Humans eat

---

12 A number of internet sites were researched to accumulate this information:
- http://www.scientificamerican.com/article.cfm?id=does-stress-feed-cancer,
- http://www.lamarfreed.net/stressandms.html,
- http://www.everydayhealth.com/crohns-disease/crohns-disease-stress.aspx,
- http://www.mayoclinic.com/health/stress/AN01286,
- http://alcoholism.about.com/cs/teens/a/blcasa030819.htm,
- http://www.guardian.co.uk/education/2008/mar/18/schools.uk8,
- http://marinecorpstimes.com/offduty/health/offduty_porn_033110/,
- http://www.divinecaroline.com/22175/109943-lying-affects-health.

13 "Dangers of Coffee Addiction," http://expertscolumn.com/content/dangers-coffee-addiction; "Effects of Caffeine on the Human Body, http://www.10tv.com/content/stories/2012/04/20/commit-caffeine-human-body.html.

these animals, not realizing that they are also consuming that adrenaline in large doses. All this is killing the body. The adrenaline high of living dangerously, sinning becomes addictive and leads to addictive behavior. [14]

As Seventh-day Adventists, we hold a unique answer to the dilemma of stress, which is in actuality "fear." The answer is found in the three angel's messages: "Fear God" (Revelation 14:6). Those who truly fear God will not live in fear of anything else. To fear God means to "keep his commandments" (Ecclesiastes 12:13), and keeping His commandments can only be done as we come to Christ. The Bible tells us "the joy of the Lord is your strength" (Nehemiah 8:10). "A merry heart doeth good like a medicine: but a broken spirit drieth the bones" (Proverbs 17:22). Is happiness a cure for disease? Even science is beginning to bear this out that it is. [15]

True happiness comes only in Christ and keeping his commandments. "Where there is no vision, the people perish: but he that keepeth the law, happy is he" (Proverbs 29:18.) In other words, where there is no hope, no vision of the future. When all is bleak and depressing, people are likely, much more likely to perish spiritually and physically than those who have merry hearts because they keep God's law and fear Him. Could this be the reason behind the promise given to ancient Israel when God said:

> If thou wilt diligently hearken to the voice of the Lord thy God, and wilt do that which is right in his sight, and wilt give ear to his commandments, and keep all his statutes, I will put none of these diseases upon thee, which I have brought upon the Egyptians: for I am the Lord that healeth thee. (Exodus 15:26)

Christ beckons us, "Come unto me, all ye that labour and are heavy laden, and I will give you rest" (Matthew 11:28). Christ crucified at the cross, showing us the only way to have peace, is the only answer to living above stress. We lay all our burdens, guilt, and fears at the foot of the cross. Negative thoughts kill. Healing must start with a purified mind. As Jesus on the cross refused vinegar, which is fermented cider, so we, by the principle of the cross, should refuse anything that defiles the mind or body.

---

14 Delialah Falcon, "Hormones in Animals and Meat Quality," http://www.steadyhealth.com/articles/Hormones_In_Animals_And_Meat_Quality_a2217.html

15 "Happiness & Health," *Harvard Public Health Review*, Harvard School of Public Health, http://www.hsph.harvard.edu/news/hphr/chronic-disease-prevention/happiness-stress-heart-disease/

A careful study of the eight laws of health reveals that they are designed to relieve stress:

1. Proper nutrition means we refrain from flesh foods that stimulate the nervous system through the release of adrenaline from the animal itself when it senses it is about to be slaughtered. [16]

2. Exercise in fresh air relieves the buildup of adrenaline. [17]

3. Water hydrates the body while dehydration prompts the release of adrenaline since the body senses it is in danger. This is just one of the reasons that caffeine appears to energize people. It is the release of adrenaline in the body as a result of the danger of being dehydrated. [18]

4. Sunshine releases endorphins that help to relieve stress. [19]

5. Temperance speaks to the issue of moderation and against addiction, which is strengthened by the "adrenaline high." [20]

6. Pure air is more important than food or water, and proper breathing is fundamental to good health. [21]

7. Rest releases endorphins while adrenaline causes restlessness. [22]

8. Trust in God is definitely the best way to unload stress. [23]

---

16 See footnote 14.

17 Fleur Hupston, "How Exercise Relieves Stress and Anxiety," http://www.naturalnews.com/028727_exercise_anxiety.html

18 "Water Relieves Stress," http://www.family-stress-relief-guide.com/water-relieves-stress.html.

19 "The Sunshine Vitamin May Reduce Stress," *Medicinal Food News*, http://www.medicinalfoodnews.com/vol03/issue7/sunshine.

20 Kevin Valeu, "Adrenaline Addiction: Sings, Symptoms, and Soteriology," http://voices.yahoo.com/adrenaline-addiction-signs-symptoms-soteriology-6208158.html?cat=5; Patrick Lencioni, "The Painful Reality of Adrenaline Addiction," http://www.leadershipreview.org/2005winter/LencioniArticle.pdf.

21 See footnote 17.

22 "Tips to Reduce Stress and Sleep Better," Sleep Disorders Health Center, http://www.webmd.com/sleep-disorders/tips-reduce-stress.

23 Debra Williams, "Scientific Research of Prayer: Can the Power of Prayer Be Proven?" http://www.plim.org/PrayerDeb.htm; "Seniors Use Prayer to Cope with Stress; Prayer No. 1 Alternative Remedy," http://www.sciencedaily.com/releases/2001/01/010103113921.htm.

The cross is the best place to unload our burdens, so it is the true starting place for healing. The medical field uses a serpent on a pole to symbolize healing. As God's people, we must direct the sick to the true serpent on the pole, Christ lifted up (see John 3:14). Every facet of our message should be connected with the cross. When this becomes the case, then God will turn up the volume, amplifying the three angels' messages.

Group Project Discussion Questions

1. Elaborate on each section.
2. How is the cross related to the doctrinal teachings of the Bible?

Chapter 23
The Cross-centered
Three Angels' Messages

T he Bible tells us that the three angels' messages will go forth with great power under the latter rain. For more than 160 years, we have been preaching the three angels' messages, yet without the power we know is to come. The glory and power of Revelation 18:1 is understood to be Christ and Him crucified adding freshness, sweetness, and power to the message. The sincere and true-hearted Christians found in the fallen churches will be drawn to a cross-centered truth— the missing ingredient in our message. The reason that another angel will descend is to help a church that believes she is rich in truth and has everything she needs to finish the work. The angel will enlighten God's people concerning His glory and power. This chapter will look at three angels' messages in light of that other angel, the new light of the old rugged cross.

The Cross and the First Angel's Message

> I saw another angel fly in the midst of heaven, having the ever-lasting gospel to preach unto them that dwell on the earth, and to every nation, and kindred, and tongue, and people, saying with a loud voice, Fear God, and give glory to him; for the hour of his judgment is come: and worship him that made heaven, and earth, and the sea, and the fountains of waters. (Revelation 14:6, 7)

- *Everlasting Gospel*
  The commission of the first angel is to take the "everlasting gospel" to every nation, kindred and tongue, and people. Everything subsequent in the first angel's message is to direct our minds and the minds of our hearers back to the "everlasting gospel." Ellen White tells us exactly what that gospel is.

> Hanging upon the cross Christ was the gospel. Now we have a message, "Behold the Lamb of God, which taketh away the sins of the world." Will not our church members keep their eyes fixed on a crucified and risen Saviour, in whom their hopes of eternal life are centered? This is our message, our argument, our

doctrine, our warning to the impenitent, our encouragement for the sorrowing, the hope for every believer. If we can awaken an interest in men's minds that will cause them to fix their eyes on Christ, we may step aside, and ask them only to continue to fix their eyes upon the Lamb of God. They thus receive their lesson. Whosoever will come after Me, let him deny himself, and take up his cross, and follow Me. He whose eyes are fixed on Jesus will leave all. He will die to selfishness. He will believe in all the Word of God, which is so gloriously and wonderfully exalted in Christ. (*Manuscript Releases*, vol. 21, 37)

Our challenge is to spread the message of "Christ hanging upon the tree" to the whole world. Many Christians have a faulty concept of the cross and what it stands for. The everlasting gospel is to clear up the confusion and reveal the correct understanding of what Christ's death accomplished. God's people will go forth with the new light of the old rugged cross.

The cross of Calvary challenges, and will finally vanquish every earthly and hellish power. In the cross all influence centers, and from it all influence goes forth. It is the great center of attraction; for on it Christ gave up His life for the human race. This sacrifice was offered for the purpose of restoring man to his original perfection; yea, more. It was offered to give him an entire transformation of character, making him more than a conqueror. ...

Christ declared, "I, if I be lifted up, ... will draw all men unto me." If the cross does not find an influence in its favor, it creates an influence. Through generation succeeding generation, the truth for this time is revealed as present truth. Christ on the cross was the medium whereby mercy and truth met together, and righteousness and peace kissed each other. This is the means that is to move the world. ("Following Christ," *The General Conference Bulletin*, April 1, 1899)

The first angel's message is designed to move the world. Many will be moved from Babylon into the truth, once we lift up Christ and Him crucified.

- ***Fear God***
  The angel next draws our attention to the issue of fearing God. The fear of the Lord is the beginning of wisdom: a good understanding

have all they that do his commandments: his praise endureth for ever" (Psalm 111:10).

In other words, to fear the Lord is equivalent to becoming wise. The angel's call to fear the Lord is a call to stop living, behaving and believing foolishly so that we can become wise. But how is that accomplished? Paul tells us. "But we preach Christ crucified, unto the Jews a stumbling block, and unto the Greeks foolishness; but unto them which are called, both Jews and Greeks, Christ the power of God, and the wisdom of God" (1 Corinthians 1:23, 24). The wisdom of God is attainable through the cross of Christ.

The cross makes us wise concerning the truth. Many are confused and know not what to believe about the gospel. The cross, in connection with the three angels' messages, will clear up that confusion. The call to fear God is, therefore, a life-and-death call. To reject the true meaning of the cross is to reject the wisdom of God. Those who continue to foolishly trust in Babylon, not fearing God or His truth, must perish in their sins. "Many shall be purified, and made white, and tried; but the wicked shall do wickedly: and none of the wicked shall understand; but the wise shall understand" (Daniel 12:10).

- **Give Glory to Him**

The angel next calls for humanity to glorify God. But how this done? "Let your light so shine before men, that they may see your good works, and glorify your Father which is in heaven" (Matthew 5:16). The call to fear God is a call to become wise in understanding through the cross. The call to glorify God is to let that wisdom shine out through our actions. It's one thing to know the truth, it's another to live it.

We must live godly lives. But how is *that* accomplished? Paul told us that it is through the cross. "I am crucified with Christ: nevertheless I live; yet not I, but Christ liveth in me: and the life which I now live in the flesh I live by the faith of the Son of God, who loved me, and gave himself for me" (Galatians 2:20). This is why Paul refused to "glory" in anything save the cross. "God forbid that I should glory, save in the cross of our Lord Jesus Christ, by whom the world is crucified unto me, and I unto the world" (Galatians 6:14) .It is by the cross that we become crucified to this world, that old man dies, and the spiritual man is born.

The principle of the cross is obedience. To glorify God is synonymous with letting the light of the gospel shine through us. These "works" are not our own but a result of Christ in us. Hearers are to understand that faith without works is dead, and that faith, true faith in Christ's sacrifice, will lead to actions so as to prove that our faith to be genuine.

- ### *Hour of His Judgment*

The angel proceeds to bring our minds to the fact that judgment hour has already begun, a reference understood as pointing to 1844. This message, in order to have maximum effect, must point us back to the blood of the sacrifice, the cleansing agent on the antitypical Day of Atonement. That cleansing blood also reminds us of the story of the exodus out of Egypt. As God's people were called to apply the blood upon the doorposts of their houses, so the angel is sending a warning to the earth. Only those who have been covered by the blood, by the cross of Christ, will be spared by the destroying angel.

As Egypt's refusal to obey God and refusal to let the people of God go to worship Him brought about the plagues, so Babylon's refusal to obey the law of God, and their refusal to let the people of God worship and spread the three angels' messages will bring about the destruction of this world. The cause is the breaking of the law; the remedy is the blood of the Lamb. "They overcame him by the blood of the Lamb" (Revelation 12:11).

- ### *The Sabbath Truth*

The angel ends his message with the call to worship Him who made the heavens and the earth, which is a direct reference to the Sabbath. Therefore, the Sabbath must be understood and preached in relation to the cross of Christ. Ellen White said, "At the commencement of the time of trouble, we were filled with the Holy Ghost as we went forth and proclaimed the Sabbath more fully" (*Maranatha*, 170).

The children of Israel who were delivered from Egyptian captivity were first instructed on the Sabbath in Exodus 16. In the same way, those who are coming out of Babylon were similarly instructed. The parallel reveals an amazing truth about the Sabbath in connection with the sacrifice of Christ.

God told Moses that He would rain down manna from heaven a certain rate every day, but on the sixth day, He would rain down a double portion. On the seventh day, the Sabbath, no manna would be given at all. What was the lesson God wanted convey concerning the Sabbath? The people were to reveal whether or not they trusted in the provision, the double portion, given to them on the sixth day. Everything they needed to keep them for two days was given to them on the sixth day. The Sabbath was simply a sign, a practical test, to demonstrate their trust in the provision. To go out on the seventh day was equivalent to telling God that they did not trust in His provision.

When Jesus came in the flesh, He used the manna to describe Himself. "Your fathers did eat manna in the wilderness, and are dead. This is the bread which cometh down from heaven, that a man may eat thereof, and not die. I am the living bread which came down from heaven: if any man eat of this bread, he shall live for ever: and the bread that I will give is my flesh, which I will give for the life of the world" (John 6:49–51).

Jesus, our Manna, broken for us, died on the sixth day of the week. "That day was the preparation, and the sabbath drew on" (Luke 23:54). Humanity received a double portion, the full provision of salvation through the death of Christ. On Friday, the Preparation Day, every man, woman, and child must travel by faith and eat of that Manna broken for us.

The Sabbath in redemption is simply a test intended to demonstrate our trust in the provision made for us at the cross. The keeping of the Sabbath is the sign that we are truly resting in Christ. "There remaineth therefore a rest to the people of God. For he that is entered into his rest, he also hath ceased from his own works, as God did from his" (Hebrews 4:9, 10).

Resting in Christ means resting from our own works. What are our own works? "Now the works of the flesh are manifest, which are these; adultery, fornication, uncleanness, lasciviousness, idolatry, witchcraft, hatred, variance, emulations, wrath, strife, seditions, heresies, envyings, murders, drunkenness, revellings, and such like: of the which I tell you before, as I have also told you in time past, that they which do such things shall not inherit the kingdom of God" (Galatians 5:19–21) Jesus called those not resting in Him, "workers of iniquity" (Luke 13:27). All who go to Christ and fully trust in Him will no longer be workers of iniquity (lawbreakers) but keepers of the law, part of which is the Seventh-day Sabbath, a sign that we have truly accepted the cross of Christ.

The Cross and the Second Angel's Message

> There followed another angel, saying, Babylon is fallen, is fallen, that great city, because she made all nations drink of the wine of the wrath of her fornication. (Revelation 14:8)

The second angel follows the first with a message of warning. The warning is focused on the wine of Babylon. The errors of the apostate systems are to be revealed, but once again, outside of its connection with the cross, the sincere and truthful may not see the connection.

The cup of Babylon is in all actuality a counterfeit of "something genuine." Remember that Jesus gave His church a cup at the last supper. "He took the cup, and gave thanks, and gave it to them, saying, Drink ye all of it; for this is my blood of the new testament, which is shed for many for the remission of sins" (Matthew 26:27, 28). This cup, filled with unfermented grape juice, was symbolic of the New Testament, or covenant, which the book of Hebrews tells us is the law of God. Therefore, the law of God has been sealed, or confirmed, by the blood of the Lamb (see Hebrews 8:8–10). The wine is unfermented because it represents the pure covenant, the unfiltered gospel, the cleansing blood, and saving sacrifice of Christ.

Mystery Babylon also has a cup. *This* cup is full of fermented wine. It is a counterfeit of the cross and the covenant for which the cross stands. The cup represents a counterfeit version of the covenant, one mingled with truth and error. This cup is being pushed by Mystery Babylon and her harlot daughters.

Interestingly enough, the Bible tells us why we should stay away from women who push wine. "Give not thy strength unto women, nor thy ways to that which destroyeth kings. It is not for kings, O Lemuel, it is not for kings to drink wine; nor for princes strong drink: Lest they drink, and forget the law, and pervert the judgment of any of the afflicted" (Proverbs 31:3–5). The kings of the earth have become drunk with the wine of these false churches. The false churches are pushing a cup that says "forget": forget the covenant, forget the law. Even more specifically, one who drinks of this cup is encouraged to "forget" what God said to "remember": "remember the sabbath day, to keep it holy" (Exodus 20:8).

This counterfeit blood is being pushed by Babylon. In response God's people are called to enter into the largest organized blood drive this world has ever seen in an effort to present and give the true blood of Christ "to every nation, and kindred, and tongue, and people" (Revelation 14:6). Many have put a counterfeit blood on their doorposts, thinking they will be protected. Our mission is to lead God's sincere people to put down the cup, cease to be confused spiritual alcoholics who hold contradictory positions, pick up the true cup of the covenant, and put the true blood upon their doorposts, thus escaping the destruction of Babylon. Read it again.

> After these things I saw another angel come down from heaven, having great power; and the earth was lightened with his glory. And he cried mightily with a strong voice, saying, Babylon the great is fallen, is fallen, and is become the habitation of devils, and the hold of every foul spirit, and a cage of every unclean and hateful bird. For all nations have drunk of the wine of the wrath of her fornication, and the kings of the earth have committed fornication with her, and the merchants of the earth are waxed rich through the abundance of her delicacies. And I heard another voice from heaven, saying, Come out of her, my people,

that ye be not partakers of her sins, and that ye receive not of her plagues. (Revelation 18:1–4)

The Cross and the Third Angel's Message

The third angel followed them, saying with a loud voice, If any man worship the beast and his image, and receive his mark in his forehead, or in his hand, The same shall drink of the wine of the wrath of God, which is poured out without mixture into the cup of his indignation; and he shall be tormented with fire and brimstone in the presence of the holy angels, and in the presence of the Lamb: And the smoke of their torment ascendeth up for ever and ever: and they have no rest day nor night, who worship the beast and his image, and whosoever receiveth the mark of his name. Here is the patience of the saints: here are they that keep the commandments of God, and the faith of Jesus. (Revelation 14:9–12)

The third angel's message is warning against receiving the mark of the beast. For some people who have heard that the mark of the beast is Sunday worship, they cannot seem to see the significance of such a teaching. Honest and sincere as they may be, they wonder why this would be such an abomination to God. Until the mark is presented in connection with the cross of Christ, it will not have its intended effect.

• *The Mark*
The mark of the beast is a mark of rebellion, a sign of God's disapproval. The first man ever marked in Scripture was Cain. The story of Cain and Abel is a fitting illustration of who will be thus marked, and why. God required a sacrifice for the forgiveness of sins. Abel, a keeper of sheep, offered a lamb, a blood sacrifice pointing forward to the sacrifice of Christ. Cain, on the other hand, offered the fruit of his own labor, representing a bloodless sacrifice. By faithlessness he had rejected the required sacrifice, the cross of Christ.

The same will be true of those who are marked in the last days. They will be marked because of their bloodless sacrifice, their denial of the cross. Understand that, like Cain, these will claim to be worshipping God, but they will give to God what is most convenient for them. The issue of Sabbath versus Sunday may seem as insignificant as eating from one tree versus another.

However, like Abel, the "wise" will understand. They will see that it is not the size of disobedience, but the spirit of disobedience that matters with God. It was a simple test the put Adam and Eve out of the garden; it will be a simple test that again gives man right to tree of life (see Revelation 22:14). Those who decide to go along with the enforced Sunday worship do so because they do not want to go through the trials associated with picking up the cross and the loss of friends and family, convenience, and comfort. The Sabbath in connection with the cross will be "an inconvenient truth."

• *The Patience of the Saints*
   The third angel's message ends with this call for "the patience of the saints." Romans 5:3 tells us that "tribulation worketh patience." Without tribulation, we cannot learn patience or endurance. Cross-training gives the saints endurance, so said Peter: "Beloved, think it not strange concerning the fiery trial which is to try you, as though some strange thing happened unto you: But rejoice, inasmuch as ye are partakers of Christ's sufferings; that, when his glory shall be revealed, ye may be glad also with exceeding joy" (1 Peter 4:12, 13).

   Partaking of Christ's suffering is partaking of the cross. This is true cross-training. The third angel's message calls for a people to begin cross training because only "he that endureth to the end shall be saved" (Matthew 10:22). By keeping the commandments of God and the faith of Jesus when times are easy, we train to keep them when times get really hard, but training must begin now. We have not one day to lose. The world is waiting on us, waiting for the loud cry.

Group Project Activities

1. Elaborate on each section.
2. How is the cross related to the three angels' messages?

Chapter 24
Going Global—Ezekiel's Wheel

The early church experienced the early rain. The outpouring was local because the people of God were all in one place. The latter rain differs in that it will be a global outpouring. In a dream Ellen White "seemed to be in a large gathering. One of authority was addressing the company, before whom was spread out a map of the world. He said that the map pictured God's vineyard, which must be cultivated. As light from heaven shone upon any one, that one was to reflect the light to others. Lights were to be kindled in many places, and from these lights still other lights were to be kindled" (*Evangelism*, 43).

> I saw jets of light shining from cities and villages, and from the high places and the low places of the earth. God's Word was obeyed, and as a result there were memorials for Him in every city and village. His truth was proclaimed throughout the world. (*Testimonies for the Church*, vol. 9, 28)

> I saw another mighty angel commissioned to descend to the earth, to unite his voice with the third angel, and give power and force to his message. A work of worldwide extent and unwonted power is here foretold. (*The Faith I Live By*, 335)

All over the world, truth is to go forth, but this cannot happen while God's people have no unity. We must be of one accord, though in separate places. The importance of unity in God's church may best be understood in the light of an incredible vision given to the prophet Ezekiel.

Ezekiel's Vision

> And I looked, and, behold, a whirlwind came out of the north, a great cloud, and a fire infolding itself, and a brightness was about it, and out of the midst thereof as the colour of amber, out of the midst of the fire. Also out of the midst thereof came the likeness of four living creatures. (Ezekiel 1:4, 5)

After giving a description of these four beasts, his attention is the turned to another amazing sight.

> Now as I beheld the living creatures, behold one wheel upon the earth by the living creatures, with his four faces ... and their appearance and their work was as it were a wheel in the middle of a wheel. (Ezekiel 1:15, 16)

This must have been a dizzying vision. It is evident that while the creatures hovered in the atmosphere above, the wheels within the wheels moved upon the earth. Ezekiel notes how they moved in perfect sync.

> When the living creatures went, the wheels went by them: and when the living creatures were lifted up from the earth, the wheels were lifted up. Whithersoever the spirit was to go, they went, thither was their spirit to go; and the wheels were lifted up over against them: for the spirit of the living creature was in the wheels. When those went, these went; and when those stood, these stood; and when those were lifted up from the earth, the wheels were lifted up over against them: for the spirit of the living creature was in the wheels. (Ezekiel 1:19–21)

The point that stands out here is the unison of activity between the living creatures in heaven, and the work of the wheels within the wheels on earth. Many commentators liken this vision to the work of the church on earth in harmony with the work of angels in heaven for the salvation of man.

Ellen White's Comments

> The sixth chapter of Isaiah has a deep and important lesson for every one of God's workmen. Study it with humility and earnest prayer. The first and second chapters of Ezekiel should also be carefully studied. The wheels within wheels represented in this symbol was confusion to the finite eye. But a hand of infinite wisdom was revealed amid the wheels. Perfect order is brought out of the confusion. Every wheel works in its right place, in perfect harmony with every other part of the machinery.

> I have been shown that human beings desire too much power. They desire to control, and the Lord God, the mighty worker is left out of their work. The workmen feel qualified to hold the

highest place. Let no man attempt to manage that work which should be left in the hands of the great I AM, and who is in His own way planning how the work shall be done. Know that God is the Instructor of His servants, and He will work through whom He will. (*Christian Leadership*, 26)

God often uses the simplest means to accomplish the greatest results. It is His plan that every part of His work shall depend on every other part, as a wheel within a wheel, all acting in harmony. (*The Desire of Ages*, 822)

Those who have many talents and those who have few are to work unitedly, as a wheel within a wheel. (*Medical Ministry*, 201)

The Problem

In light of the above references to the wheel within the wheel, Jesus' prayer that God's will "be done, on earth, as it is in heaven" begins to make sense in the context of the latter rain. The disciples were not only of "one accord" with one another, but they were also in alignment with the work and desire of the angels in heaven. The broken wheel of disunion had been fixed *ready to move* in perfect sync with the angelic workers of heaven—the unity that existed among angels was demonstrated among the disciples at Pentecost—and the rain came as result.

No longer were they a collection of independent units or discordant, conflicting elements. No longer were their hopes set on worldly greatness. They were of "one accord," "of one heart and of one soul." Acts. 2:46; 4:32. Christ filled their thoughts; the advancement of His kingdom was their aim. (*The Acts of the Apostles*, 45)

Reflect on this for a moment. We have many ministries in our church working in their own corner, "doing their own thing" as earnestly as they can. Could it be that the devil knows that "the secret of our success in the work of God will be found in the harmonious working of our people," and that "there must be concentrated action" (*The Review and Herald*, December 2, 1890)?

Every member of the body of Christ must act his part in the cause of God, according to the ability that God has given him" and that "if Christians were to act in concert, moving forward as one, under the direction of one Power, for the accomplishment of one purpose, they would move the world" (*The Review and Herald*, December 2, 1890)

Think of the many independent wheels in the church all doing their own thing. How many ministries, for fear of their own reputation, refuse to be associated with other ministries in doing "the work of the Lord"? How many ministries struck with the "super-watchman" bug spend considerable effort seeking out faults in other ministries? Think of all the division we have. Separate conferences based on color barriers, ministries in controversy with one another or the church, the liberal wheel, the conservative wheel—it seems we've all got our own clicks, our own circles, and those who are not in our circle are viewed with suspicion. Could it be that God is waiting for the only wheel that really counts, the great wheel of the church working in harmony with heaven under the baptism of the Holy Spirit to be fixed?

The Cure

The question might be asked, "Do we unite with error for the sake of unity?" The answer is no. How then are we to unite? Study this striking illustration given by Ellen White.

Picture a large circle, from the edge of which are many lines all running to the center. The nearer these lines approach the center, the nearer they are to one another. Thus it is in the Christian life. The closer we come to Christ, the nearer we shall be to one another. God is glorified as His people unite in harmonious action. (*The Adventist Home*, 179)

The closer we come to Christ, the more willing we are to lay aside the errors that cause separation. When God's people are found "running to the center," we will see the wheel within the wheel begin to operate effectively. The opposite is true as well. The further we are from Christ, the more division and independent action there will be. Christ is the great Hub, the great Center of attraction. As we lift up His sacrifice, and make it the center, all other things fall in place. The wheel is fixed as we fix our focus upon Christ and His sacrifice. At the cross, the glory of man is humbled in the dust, and the one great aim consumes God's people. No longer will the questions be "Who is the greatest? Who will get the credit for the work done?"

In spite of all the good qualities a man may have, he cannot be a good soldier if he acts independently of those connected with him. Occasional and uncertain movements, however earnest and energetic, will in the end bring defeat. Take a strong team of horses. If, instead of both pulling together, one should suddenly jerk forward and the other pull back, they would not move the load, notwithstanding their great strength. So the soldiers of Christ must work in concert, else there will be a mere concourse of independent atoms. Strength, instead of being carefully treasured to meet one great end, will be wasted in disconcerted, meaningless efforts. In union is strength. (*The Signs of the Times*, September 7, 1891)

God designs that His people shall be a unit, that they shall see eye to eye and be of the same mind and of the same judgment. This cannot be accomplished without a clear, pointed, living testimony in the church. The prayer of Christ was that His disciples might be one as He was one with His Father. "Neither pray I for these alone, but for them also which shall believe on Me through their word; that they all may be one; as Thou, Father, art in Me, and I in Thee, that they also may be one in Us: that the world may believe that Thou hast sent Me. And the glory which Thou gavest Me I have given them; that they may be one, even as We are one: I in them, and Thou in Me, that they may be made perfect in one; and that the world may know that Thou hast sent Me, and hast loved them, as Thou hast loved Me. (*Testimonies for the Church*, vol. 3, 361)

This is how the world is to know that Jesus has been sent by God when they see the church of God moving in one purpose, a wheel within a wheel, a "unit" revealing the glory of Jesus to the world. Speaking of the latter rain and its effect upon the saints, the servant of the Lord saw a "company," "clothed with an armor from their head to their feet" who "moved in exact order, like a company of soldiers" (*Early Writings*, 271). Now is our opportunity to fix the broken wheel.

"By thousands of voices, all over the earth, the warning will be given" (*The Great Controversy*, 612). While the wheel is broken, we cannot expect rain in full measure. There is no need to reinvent the wheel, only to fix it. On September 11, 2001, in light of the impending danger aboard *United* Airlines flight 93, passenger Todd Beamer joined fellow passengers in a heroic and successful effort to overthrow the terrorists who had hijacked the plane. The last words he spoke to fellow passengers have now become famous—"Let's Roll!"

The Seventh-day Adventist church would do well to learn a lesson. Ours is no suicide mission. We are guaranteed victory but only as we are *united*. Broken wheels don't roll. They don't go anywhere. It has been more than 160 years since 1844, and more than 120 years since 1888. It's time to fix the wheel. Let's roll!

Group Discussion Questions

1. How important is it to catch the vision of global simultaneous action?

2. What can be done to advance such a vision around the world?

3. What can you do as an individual or church to accomplish the vision?

4. What impacted you most from this chapter?

Chapter 25
Operation Jericho—
a Plan to Cross the Jordan

This chapter lays out a plan for crossing the Jordan, a plan to encourage the people of God to prepare themselves for united, simultaneous action and that will call the attention of the world to the three angels' messages. It is a three-staged plan summarized as:

1. **Small evangelistic units**

2. **Global prayer**

3. **Simultaneous global evangelistic series**

---

1. Small Evangelistic Units

The first stage of the plan is to begin to form small groups of between five and eight people who will commit to gathering together at a scheduled time to study and pray together. The purpose of their gathering is to ask God how that unit may be used to reach their community. In order to do this, each unit must be equipped to learn how to study the Bible as well as how to pray. Imagine a church full of these small units, each unit devising ways to spread the gospel in their communities, each doing some form of weekly outreach to their neighborhoods. Now image these small units multiplying around the world church. Ellen White wrote, "The formation of small companies as a basis of Christian effort has been presented to me by One who cannot err." (*Testimonies for the Church*, vol. 7, 21, 22).

These units differ from the typical small group whose main purpose is fellowship and Bible study. While the activities of a small group should include these things, its main goal should be to plan how it can reach the community. When pastors of the local congregation choose a number of unit leaders, the unit leaders, in turn, choose people from the church to become part of their unit. Each individual unit will meet to discuss different ideas for evangelism. The units should plan to meet all together every couple of months to share testimonies and ideas in order to advance the message. Where a pastor is not available, the members of the church can form their own units to work in strengthening the church.

The combination of a revival in prayer and Bible study will bring about the glory of God, the rain that is to cover the earth. To learn more about these units, you can visit http://www.armebiblecamp.com/a-units.html.

Revival of Bible Study and the Latter Rain

When studying the revival of Acts 2, many are led to think that the revival was simply a result of the prayer that took place during the ten days in the upper room. While prayer was indeed one aspect of the revival, the revival had, in fact, begun earlier than Acts, chapter 2. The revival really began in Luke 24 where we find the account of the two disciples on their way to Emmaus shortly after Jesus' death and resurrection.

> Behold, two of them went that same day to a village called Emmaus, which was from Jerusalem about threescore furlongs. And they talked together of all these things which had happened. And it came to pass, that, while they communed together and reasoned, Jesus himself drew near, and went with them. But their eyes were holden that they should not know him. And he said unto them, What manner of communications are these that ye have one to another, as ye walk, and are sad? And the one of them, whose name was Cleopas, answering said unto him, Art thou only a stranger in Jerusalem, and hast not known the things which are come to pass there in these days? And he said unto them, What things? And they said unto him, Concerning Jesus of Nazareth, which was a prophet mighty in deed and word before God and all the people: And how the chief priests and our rulers delivered him to be condemned to death, and have crucified him. But we trusted that it had been he which should have redeemed Israel: and beside all this, to day is the third day since these things were done. Yea, and certain women also of our company made us astonished, which were early at the sepulchre; And when they found not his body, they came, saying, that they had also seen a vision of angels, which said that he was alive. And certain of them which were with us went to the sepulchre, and found it even so as the women had said: but him they saw not. Then he said unto them, O fools, and slow of heart to believe all that the prophets have spoken: Ought not Christ to have suffered these things, and to enter into his glory? And beginning at Moses and all the prophets, he expounded unto them in all the Scriptures the things concerning himself. And they drew nigh unto the village, whither they went: and he made as though he would have gone further. But they constrained him, saying,

Abide with us: for it is toward evening, and the day is far spent. And he went in to tarry with them. And it came to pass, as he sat at meat with them, he took bread, and blessed it, and brake, and gave to them. And their eyes were opened, and they knew him; and he vanished out of their sight. And they said one to another, Did not our heart burn within us, while he talked with us by the way, and while he opened to us the Scriptures? (Luke 24:13–32)

This is where it all began. When Jesus drew near and opened the Scriptures showing the disciples the things pertaining to Himself, their hearts began to burn. This is where the fire of Acts 2 really began, and it was as a result of Bible study.

The church of God is in need of revival today. Like the early rain (the outpouring of the Holy Spirit on the Day of Pentecost), the latter rain must be accompanied by a revival in our understanding of the Scriptures. This understanding of the teachings (doctrines) of God will play in connection with the final outpouring.

Give ear, O ye heavens, and I will speak; and hear, O earth, the words of my mouth. My doctrine shall drop as the rain, my speech shall distil as the dew, as the small rain upon the tender herb, and as the showers upon the grass. (Deuteronomy 32:1, 2)

God promises that his "doctrine" shall be poured out upon the grass: "Ask ye of the Lord rain in the time of the latter rain; so the Lord shall make bright clouds, and give them showers of rain, to every one grass in the field" (Zechariah 10:1).

Each individual is like a blade of grass and God is waiting to pour his rain upon us.

Currently, the Seventh-day Adventist Church is comprised of 16.3 million blades of "grass" worldwide. When each blade, each individual realizes that he or she too can play a part in the outpouring of the Spirit, that his or her personal revival *will* come when he or she begins to study the Bible and pray like never before, revival will supernaturally take place. Each of us, as individuals, must realize that God is waiting to instill revival individually as well as corporately. Christ will draw near to you and to me to grant us "heartburn."

A revival in Bible study is needed throughout the world. Attention is to be called, not to the assertions of men, but to the Word of God. As this is done, a mighty work will be wrought. When God declared that His Word should not return unto Him

204 | The Coming Oil Crisis

void, He meant all that He said. The gospel is to be preached to all nations. The Bible is to be opened to the people. A knowledge of God is the highest education, and it will cover the earth with its wonderful truth as the waters cover the sea. (*Evangelism*, 456)

2. Global Prayer [24]

The second stage of the Operation Jericho is for the people of God to unite globally to seek God's face in prayer. In the year 2007, 1,850 churches from eighty-three countries united in ten days of prayer to seek the outpouring of the Holy Spirit in the latter rain. That event was the beginning of Operation Global Rain. God is now moving to fix the broken wheel of disunity among His people. It is in united prayer that God's people prepare the way for the outpouring of the Spirit. This global gathering in many places at one time is critical to the receiving of the latter rain. "Could there be a convocation of all the churches of earth, the object of their united cry should be for the Holy Spirit." (*Manuscript Releases*, 24)

The circumstances may seem to be favorable for a rich outpouring of the showers of grace. But God himself must command the rain to fall. Therefore we should not be remiss in supplication. We are not to trust to the ordinary working of providence. We must pray that God will unseal the fountain of the water of life. And we must ourselves receive of the living water. Let us, with contrite hearts, pray most earnestly that now, in the time of the latter rain, the showers of grace may fall upon us. At every meeting we attend, our prayers should ascend that at this very time, God will impart warmth and moisture to our souls. As we seek God for the Holy Spirit, it will work in us meekness, humbleness of mind, a conscious dependence upon God for the perfecting latter rain. If we pray for the blessing in faith, we shall receive it as God has promised. (*The Review and Herald*, March 2, 1897)

A revival of true godliness among us is the greatest and most urgent of all our needs. To seek this should be our first work. There must be earnest effort to obtain the blessing of the Lord, not because God is not willing to bestow His blessing upon us, but because we are unprepared to receive it. Our heavenly Father is more willing to give His Holy Spirit to them that ask Him, than are earthly parents to give good gifts to their children. But it is our work, by confession, humiliation, repentance, and earnest

---

24 To learn more about Operation Global Rain, visit
www.revivalandreformation.org.

prayer, to fulfill the conditions upon which God has promised to grant us His blessing. A revival need be expected only in answer to prayer. (*Selected Messages*, Book 1, 121)

Thousands of people around the world are joining in this global appeal to the God of heaven for the outpouring of His Spirit. How it will take in its fullness is yet to be seen. Like Elijah, our faith will surely be tried. Ellen White speaking of this said:

It was not because of any outward evidence that the showers were about to fall, that Elijah could so confidently bid Ahab prepare for rain. The prophet saw no clouds in the heavens; he heard no thunder. He simply spoke the word that the Spirit of the Lord had moved him to speak in response to his own strong faith.... Having done all that was in his power to do, he knew that Heaven would freely bestow the blessings foretold. The same God who had sent the drought had promised an abundance of rain as the reward of rightdoing; and now Elijah waited for the promised outpouring. In an attitude of humility, "his face between his knees," he interceded with God in behalf of penitent Israel. ...

Six times the servant returned with the word that there was no sign of rain in the brassy heavens. Undaunted, Elijah sent him forth once more; and this time the servant returned with the word, "Behold, there ariseth a little cloud out of the sea, like a man's hand. (*Conflict and Courage*, 211)

We must be earnest and patient in prayer.

The answer may come with sudden velocity and overpowering might; or it may be delayed for days and weeks, and our faith receive a trial. But God knows how and when to answer our prayer. It is our part of the work to put ourselves in connection with the divine channel. God is responsible for *his* part of the work. He is faithful who hath promised. The great and important matter with us is to be of one heart and mind, putting aside all envy and malice, and, as humble supplicants, to watch and wait. Jesus, our Representative and Head, is ready to do for us what he did for the praying, watching ones on the day of Pentecost. (*The Spirit of Prophecy*, vol. 3, 272, 273)

3. Simultaneous Global Evangelistic Series

In the political field "the ground game" is a term used to define the tactics used by each candidate in order to win as many votes as possible. As Adventists, we too should have a ground game for the three angels' messages, a calculated plan of action to mobilize the grassroots of the church to act. Imagine a simultaneous evangelistic meeting so extensive, so broad that it grabbed the attention of every nation. It could happen, if the meetings were being held globally by thousands of churches around the world, advertising the same theme.

If we consider our mission in military language, the concept becomes even more crystal clear. The general of an army has no power if he cannot mobilize his army to act. If there is no clear channel of communication, the president's commands are useless. The chain of command and communication is critical to the success of any mission.

> I was shown that ministers of Christ should discipline themselves for the warfare. Greater wisdom is required in generalship in the work of God than is required of the generals engaged in national battles. Ministers of God's choosing are engaged in a great work. They are warring not merely against men, but against Satan and his angels. Wise generalship is required here. (*Gospel Workers*, 155)

> The leaders in God's cause, as wise generals, are to lay plans for advance moves all along the line. In their planning they are to give special study to the work that can be done by the laity for their friends and neighbors. The work of God in this earth can never be finished until the men and women comprising our church membership rally to the work, and unite their efforts with those of ministers and church officers. (*Gospel Workers*, 351, emphasis added)

Imagine a meeting where thousands of lay people from every nation prepare to deliver the message of the three angels at the same time. Imagine that on billboards all around the world in different languages is an invitation to hear a powerful series of presentation. Imagine that the title of the presentation is the same in every language. On billboards, TV advertisements, radio, and t-shirts this title and date would be visible for all to see.

The meetings would start on the same date around the world, and the message would be delivered by lay people, evangelists, pastors, and church administrators. The message would be focused on the contents of the Ark of the Covenant and centered on the righteousness of Christ as well as the cross-centered three angels' messages.

The message would encourage the people to clear the way to prepare for the coming of Jesus. It would reveal the wine of Babylon. It would call people to come out of her. It would, indeed, be an unprecedented event. What a *loud sound* that would make around the world. I believe that sound could be so loud that it could indeed be the LOUD cry!

Yes, it would attract the attention of the world in a good way, but also in a bad way. Many church leaders would be angered as they saw their flock deserting them for the truth of the Scriptures, and yes, Adventism would most definitely be on the map. We would be noticed, and more than that, persecuted. It would lead most certainly to the king of the north responding in great fury.

Wouldn't it be worth it though, for when that time of trouble comes as a result of such a powerful event, when the wicked seek to destroy God's people, then Michael will stand up (Daniel 12:1). We have no need to fear. We are able to go up and possess the land. We need not fear the giants. The Rahabs are waiting on us. Let us step into the water while the oil is still available.

Group Discussion Questions

1. Will we take action?

2. How?